Praise for the *Eart*

There is no doubt that this world is in crisis. The ecological and sociological reality we're living in and must face up to is quite frankly terrifying. Yet there is hope. The authors of the *Earth Spirit* series from Moon Books show us that there are solutions to be found in ecological and eco-spiritual practices. I recommend this series to anyone who is concerned about our current situation and wants to find some hope in solutions they can practice for themselves.
Sarah Kerr, Pagan Federation President

This bold and rich *Earth Spirit* series provides vital information, perspectives, poetry and wisdom to guide and support through the complex environmental, climate and biodiversity challenges and crisis facing us all. Nothing is avoided within the wide range of author views, expertise and recommendations on eco-spirituality. I am deeply inspired by the common call, across the books, to radically change our relationship with the planet to a more respectful, mutual, spiritual and sustainable way of living; both individually and collectively. Each book offers its own particular flavour and practical offering of solutions and ways forward in these unprecedented times. Collectively the series provides an innovative, inspiring and compelling compendium of how to live, hope and act from both ancient and modern wisdoms. Whatever your views, concerns and aspirations for your life, and for the planet, you will find something of value. My life and understanding is deeply enhanced through the privilege of reading this series.
Dr Lynne Sedgmore CBE, Founder of Goddess Luminary Leadership Wheel, Executive Coach, Priestess and ex Chief Executive

In a world that is faced with such immense environmental issues, we can often feel paralysed and impotent. The *Earth Spirit* series is a welcome and inspiring antidote to fear and apathy. These books gift us with positive and inspiring visions that serve to empower and strengthen our own resolve to contribute to the healing of our planet, our communities and ourselves.
Eimear Burke, Chosen Chief of The Order of Bards, Ovates and Druids

Thanks to Moon Books and an amazing group of authors for stepping up in support of our need to address, with grace and aliveness, the ecological crises facing humanity. We must take concerted, focused, positive action on every front NOW, and this is best and most powerfully done when we base our offerings in a deep sense of spirit. White Buffalo Woman came to us 20 generations ago, reminding us of the importance of a holy perception of the world - based in Oneness, unity, honor and respect. Even as that is profound, it is also practical, giving us a baseline of power from which to give our gifts of stewardship and make our Earth walk a sacred one - for us and for All Our Relations. Walk in Beauty with these authors!
Brooke Medicine Eagle, Earthkeeper and author of *Buffalo Woman Comes Singing* and *The Last Ghost Dance*

Earth Spirit is an exciting and timely series. It has never been more important to engage with ideas that promote a positive move forward for our world. Our planet needs books like these - they offer us heartening signposts through the most challenging of times.
Philip Carr-Gomm, author of *Druid Mysteries, Druidcraft* and *Lessons in Magic*

Our relationship to the Mother Earth and remembering our roles as caretakers and guardians of this sacred planet is essential in weaving ourselves back into the tapestry of our own sacred nature. From the shamanic perspective, we are not separate from nature. The journey to finding solutions for the Earth will come through each person's reconnection to her heartbeat and life force.
Chandra Sun Eagle, author of *Looking Back on the Future*

This is important work as we humans face one of the greatest challenges in our collective history.
Ellen Evert Hopman, Archdruid of Tribe of the Oak and author of *A Legacy of Druids, A Druid's Herbal of Sacred Tree Medicine, The Sacred Herbs of Spring,* and other volumes

What people are saying about

Earth Spirt - Gaia

As we watch what is happening to our planet, many of us succumb to "ecological grief," as Irisanya Moon describes it in *Earth Spirit - Gaia*. Our planet—Gaia—is suffering immensely from the impact of humanity. Grief or not, if we don't step up for Gaia, then... who? Irisanya offers a variety of ways to connect to Gaia personally, practices for living an Earth-friendly lifestyle and nurturing a Gaia-centric mindset, and suggestions for creating community to protect and heal Gaia right in your own neighborhood. With meditations, rituals, and group activities, Irisanya guides us toward *cultivating radical hope* that it's not too late to help our planet. With changed minds, behaviors, and choices, we can help Gaia heal.
Debra DeAngelo, author of *Pagan Curious: A Beginner's Guide to Nature, Magic & Spirituality* and *Sacred Massage: The Magic and Ritual of Soothing Touch*

The Earth is our home. When we live in relationship with her, we bring not only physical balance into our lives, but spiritual balance as well. In her latest book, *Earth Spirit - Gaia,* Irisanya Moon invites us to reconnect with the Earth, to rediscover the many gifts she offers us, and to bring our own offerings to her heart in the form of care and connection. During this time when the climate is changing and the planet is in crisis it can be easy to lose hope and disconnect from our relationship to our planet. From the history of the goddess Gaia, to magical exercises and suggestions for nurturing and tending to the Earth, Irisanya opens the door for all of us to step inside the natural world and discover the beauty and wildness that is all around. This work beckons us back to a place of action, hope and wholeness.
Emily Morrison, Wise Woman Witchery

Earth Spirit
Gaia

Saving Her, Saving Ourselves

Earth Spirit

Gaia

Saving Her, Saving Ourselves

Irisanya Moon

MOON BOOKS
Winchester, UK
Washington, USA

JOHN HUNT PUBLISHING

First published by Moon Books, 2023
Moon Books is an imprint of John Hunt Publishing Ltd., No. 3 East Street, Alresford
Hampshire SO24 9EE, UK
office@jhpbooks.net
www.johnhuntpublishing.com
www.moon-books.net

For distributor details and how to order please visit the 'Ordering' section on our website.

ISBN: 978 1 80341 108 8
978 1 80341 109 5 (ebook)
Library of Congress Control Number: 2022942426

A CIP catalogue record for this book is available from the British Library.

Design: Lapiz Digital Services

UK: Printed and bound by CPI Group (UK) Ltd, Croydon, CR0 4YY
Printed in North America by CPI GPS partners

Contents

The more we understand and know of Gaia, perhaps
the better we might care for Her.
We save ourselves by saving the goddess.

Acknowledgments

I acknowledge the land that I currently live on. The land of the Miwok, Pomo, and the Graton Rancheria peoples, the land held sacred by those who have walked, do walk, and will continue to steward the land. (If you know the peoples of your land, please acknowledge them now. If you do not, I invite you to find out.)

I also want to acknowledge those who have also written other books in the *Earth Spirit* series, with the goal of expanding awareness of eco-spirituality in its different facets and impact. Thanks, Moon Books, for seeing a place for these authors and for these messages of wisdom, hope, and warning.

I acknowledge that one book or one viewpoint is not enough to change the world, but I hope that meeting with Gaia is a place that will resonate deeply. Sometimes walking in the mythic can expand our creativity to meet old problems with a new perspective.

We need to think beyond what we know and realize that we are not separate from Earth. We too are Earth. We are saving ourselves when we save Her.[1]

Author's Note

In the Reclaiming Witchcraft tradition, the emphasis on environmental activism is one of the first things you learn. It's a part of the *Principles of Unity*, a co-created and evolving document that outlines the shared beliefs of Reclaiming Witches.

(These are pieces from the document. The rest can be found in my other *Earth Spirit* book, *Honoring the Wild: Reclaiming Witchcraft and Environmental Activism*.)

> The values of the Reclaiming tradition stem from our understanding that the earth is alive and all of life is sacred and interconnected. We see the Goddess as immanent in the earth's cycles of birth, growth, death, decay, and regeneration. Our practice arises from a deep, spiritual commitment to the earth, to healing, and to the linking of magic with political action....
>
> Our tradition honors the wild and calls for service to the earth and the community. We work in diverse ways, including nonviolent direct action, for all forms of justice: environmental, social, political, racial, gender, and economic....
>
> All living beings are worthy of respect. All are supported by the sacred elements of air, fire, water, and earth. We work to create and sustain communities and cultures that embody our values, that can help to heal the wounds of the earth and her peoples, and that can sustain us and nurture future generations.

Reclaiming Principles of Unity – Consensed by the Reclaiming Collective in 1997, then updated by consensus at the BIRCH council meeting of Dandelion Gathering 5 in 2012 and at the BIRCH Council meeting in January 2021.

I offer this to set the tone for the importance of Gaia in my own life. While I did not start as an activist witch, nor did I gaze beyond the candles and spells of various authors, witchcraft is inherently political – and so have I become. With time, age, and experience, it is impossible to deny the world's interconnectedness. By taking care of Earth, we take care of ourselves and each other.

Introduction

> *Verily at the first Chaos came to be, but next wide-bosomed Earth, the ever-sure foundations of all the deathless ones who hold the peaks of snowy Olympus, and dim Tartarus in the depth of the wide-pathed Earth, and Eros (Love), fairest among the deathless gods, who unnerves the limbs and overcomes the mind and wise counsels of all gods and all men within them. From Chaos came forth Erebus and black Night; but of Night were born Aether and Day, whom she conceived and bare from union in love with Erebus. And Earth first bare starry Heaven, equal to herself, to cover her on every side, and to be an ever-sure abiding-place for the blessed gods. And she brought forth long Hills, graceful haunts of the goddess-Nymphs who dwell amongst the glens of the hills. She bare also the fruitless deep with his raging swell, Pontus, without sweet union of love.*
>
> Translated by Evelyn-White, H G., *Hesiod, Homeric Hymns, Epic Cycle,*

To contain Gaia in a simple description or experience is impossible. Just as it is complicated and strained to contain your own birth in one sentence, describing the birth of the world (wide-bosomed Earth) begins only as it can – at the beginning.

Together, we will meet Gaia in many of Her descriptions and myths. We will journey into the depths of thought and the Gaia Hypothesis. And we will bring Her blessings to the place of the moment when you read this book.

I don't know what that moment holds for you or for Earth, or for the people who make it home. What I do know is that Earth is the place of our birth and our death. It is the place where we encounter our frailty while blossoming into our purpose. Hopefully.

This precious Earth holds it all. And I believe it is essential to our future to know Her well. To sit alongside Gaia and find ourselves to be more alike than separate. To be collaborators in the creation of new myths and new magick. We need each other. We always have.

But how can we truly meet each other in the places that are most necessary unless we know each other? There might be those who can connect with awe in a sunrise or the newly waxing moon. Others might turn to the ocean, while others hear the owls and know connection.

Gaia is also there. She is also calling. Can you answer the call?

Chapter 1

Meeting Gaia

In the beginning, there came Nothing, alone. It was sometimes called Chaos, or the Void. But it was Nothing, all the same. Next appeared Earth, so the gods would have some place to stand. And then came Tartarus, the underworld. Eros, love, came into being... Earth brought forth Heaven and Sea. Heaven was as great as Earth and spread out above and beyond Earth to cover her with stars. Heaven was a place of rest for all the gods. And then Earth gave birth to mountains--Mt. Olympus being the home of the gods.
Virginia Hamilton, *The Coming of All Things, The Greek Creators* – from *In the Beginning*

The first meditation I ever did in a coven-like setting led me to a wide goddess with white hair and a belly like a cushion. A belly like the roundness of the planet. I laid in Her lap and knew Her to be nameless as mystery but familiar as the curve of the tree in the backyard where I grew up. I was certain I'd met someone older than old. Someone who had been around at the beginning of everything. I wouldn't know until later who She was. And perhaps She was more. After all, the godds[2] are more expansive than I think we can sometimes understand.

Who Is Gaia?

Gaia (or Gaea, Gaiê, Gê) is the oldest of deities, also known as Mother Earth, the Great Goddess, or the White Goddess (Guiley 131). Born from the darkness of Chaos when the universe was formed, She desired love, so then birthed and married Her son Uranus (Ouranos), or Father Heaven, and gave birth to the Titans and Cyclops.

Gaia was the first goddess to emerge from Chaos, but this was not due to a recognition of goddesses being above male gods in the Greek pantheon hierarchy. Instead, She was the first because it was easier to believe that a female body could give birth. (Lefkowitz 14)

Gaia continued to birth beings including Pontus, the Ourea, the Hecatonchires, the Gigantes, Nereus, Thaumus, Phorcys, Ceto, Eurybia, Aergia, Typhon, Python, and Antaeus. The texts sometimes conflict about who the fathers were or if there were fathers, so I will leave them as children of Gaia. These children are said to be both wondrous and monstrous.

According to some, Gaia was (and is) an antagonist, one who seemed to be the troublemaker among the godds. She rebelled against Her son/husband and was often seen to cause problems for anyone who might upset Her. Now, this might be one of those interpretations and translations that came from one of the many male translators, which stuck as it was repeated so often.

She is considered the first to be worshipped and, according to Burkert, perhaps even a prototype for all deities and holy ones. Burkert goes on to talk about the evocation of the political as well as the agrarian aspects in the way that the land sustains and those who benefit have obligations in return (Burkert 175). Gaia was also considered the first Pythia (oracular priestess) at Delphi (Goodrich 236).

It is also wise to point out that Hesiod continuously points out the negative qualities of females in *Theogony*. At the same time, certain events would not have happened without the various interventions of the female-bodied deities (Lefkowitz 23-24).

Over time, Gaia was less and less at the forefront of worship and reverence. This does not mean there weren't cults for Her. In fact, there were cults to Gaia across Southern Greece, including Attica, Laconia, Elis, Achaea, and Arcadia. She was most often worshipped alongside Demeter, who grew in stature and importance, but usually as equals.

Titles and Epithets

I offer these titles and epithets as ways to honor Gaia in your personal practice or in more public workings with Her. I find that knowing other names and honoraries of deities helps me connect.

I can chant these names to an altar or use them as guides during meditations to get to know Gaia more. Another suggestion would be to work with different aspects of Her as they call to you.

- Anesido'ra (Anêsidôra) – spender of gifts
- Callligeneia (Kalligeneia) – a surname of Gaea
- Eurysternos (Eurusternos) – broad-chested goddess
- Gasêpton (Gasepton) – August Earth
- Khthon (Chthon) – Earth
- Khthoniê (Chthonia) – Earth
- Kourotrophos (Curotrophus) – Nurse of the Young
- Matêr Pantôn (Mater Panton) – Mother of All
- Megalê Thea (Megale Thea) – Great Goddess
- Olympia (Olympia) – of Olympia
- Pando'rus (Pandôros) – a surname of Gaia

If you continue to research these names, you will find that some of them are also related to Demeter. This makes sense as they are in the same pantheon and Demeter is the goddess of the harvest and agriculture, overseeing crops, grains, food, and the earth's fertility.[3]

The Complexities of Gaia

It is interesting to notice that many of the retellings of the world's creation in the Greek pantheon focus less on Gaia and more on the godds and humans that came after. As though Gaia was more of an instrument of creation that led to 'better' things and more 'important' beings.

Gaia was at risk of being lost. According to Patricia Monaghan, while the invading Olympians supplanted Gaia, She was still worshipped by the Greek people, given barley and honey at sacred openings on the earth. At these fissures in the land, those with the gift of prophecy would gather messages from Gaia in these places, informing the oracles of Delphi and beyond (Monaghan 131).

Also known as the wife of starry heaven, Gaia is part of a more nuanced landscape. Spretnak speaks of the Greeks seeing the earth as the home of the dead, which means the earth holds power over the spirit world. Some priestesses would sleep in holy shrines, with their ears to the ground to hear what Gaia had to say. Or they would sit over a crevice with vapors rising, go into a trance, and speak of the future (Spretnak 45).

In addition, some critique of Theogony includes the idea that Gaia might simply be a vengeful mother, someone who might be harmful to men.

> *...Gaia is a non-anthropomorphic deity with the personality of a vengeful mother, with some admirable qualities such as maternal instinct and intelligence. Although Hesiod cautions against this intelligence, illustrating it as a deadly aspect of female beings, particularly to males. He continued to reveal the less admirable qualities of women through Gaia: sporadically threatening and tremendously strong. This nature is mirrored in Gaia's actions and reactions to humans living on earth.*[4]

The nurturing and powerful images of Gaia are not always supported in the texts or in translations of the texts. Instead, there may also be an undercurrent of 'fighting' Mother Nature or trying to control Her wrath. And in thinking of this, it sets up an adversarial relationship with Mother Earth. Whether conscious or not, how does this impact our ability to care for Earth?

Exercise: Getting to Know Gaia

Because I believe experience informs relationship, and vice versa, I invite you to take a journey to meet with this being.

For this trance, it is wise to be in a comfortable space, but not so comfortable that you will fall asleep. You can choose to sit, lay down, or even walk if that feels supportive. It can help to record the following trance or to review it ahead of time to lead yourself through the journey.

Begin with finding a place of comfort. You might call attention to your breath and your body, allowing things to settle and move away from anything that came before this moment and away from anything that comes after this moment.

It might feel good to you to take a few deep breaths or just to follow your breath as it is, without trying to change it or fix it. Just settle into yourself and into your body.

It can feel helpful to travel the length of your body to release any tension, allowing you to go deeper and deeper into this place of knowing. This place of wisdom that you have within your body and mind.

Let's start with your feet and ankles, allowing your awareness to travel here and notice what is happening and how you can easily let anything unnecessary drop, sink, and fall away. (Pause)

Move along your calves and knees and up your thighs, allowing your awareness to travel here and notice what is happening and how you can easily let anything unnecessary drop, sink, and fall away. (Pause)

Travel again to the place of your pelvic bowl and hips, swirling around and between those hip bones, swirling around the place of digestion and will, allowing your awareness to travel here and notice what is happening and how you can easily let anything unnecessary drop, sink, and fall away. (Pause)

Move up and along the space of your lungs and ribs, perhaps even following each rib bone until you get to the heart and settle there, allowing your awareness to travel here and notice what is happening and how you can easily let anything unnecessary drop, sink, and fall away. (Pause)

Shifting once more along the length of your shoulders, arms, and fingers, allowing your awareness to travel here and notice what is happening and how you can easily let anything unnecessary drop, sink, and fall away. (Pause)

Traveling again, once more, you're so comfortable with this now, to the place of your neck and along your jaw. Maybe you need to unclench your jaw or move it around, allowing your awareness to travel here and notice what is happening and how you can easily let anything unnecessary drop, sink, and fall away. (Pause)

And again, moving to the place of your head, along the forehead and to the top of your head, to that place that was soft when you were born, allowing your awareness to travel here and notice what is happening and how you can easily let anything unnecessary drop, sink, and fall away. (Pause)

If there is anything else that needs to drop, sink, or fall away, let this be the moment it can happen. Easily and gently.

From this place of lightness and ease, I invite you to open the awareness at the top of your head, spreading it out like a blanket or blowing it out like a dandelion, the seeds scattering to the corners of your consciousness. Expand as far as you like and as far as you need.

In this wide-open space, I encourage you to find a path and a way. You might see it, you might feel it, you might just know it's there. Begin to follow it and know it will lead you to where you want to go, to where you need to go today.

Along this path, you might begin to notice the blessings and the wonder of the earth. What do you see? What do you feel? What do you sense? What do you recognize and what is new to your experience? Allow yourself to linger in the bounty and brightness of the earth. Or notice the decay and the whispers of life's cycle ending.

As you continue along this path, you become aware of a figure in the distance, and She is calling to you in the way that you know. By the name that She knows you by. You can travel to Her now and spend some time with this being, Gaia. If this is the first time you have met, you may have a short conversation or you might only see Her for a moment or two. Allow this meeting to be whatever it needs to be today. You can always return. (Pause for a few minutes to have an experience.)

When you feel the experience is complete, you can give thanks to Gaia, or you can simply turn to leave. Come back to the path you traveled to come to this place. Perhaps you notice new things on the way back, or things look different than they did when you first came this way. You may want to consider what you have learned and what questions you still have.

As you reach the place where you widened your awareness, draw it back in. Pull the blanket back and see the dandelion seeds flowing back to your head, as though they were reattaching. Come back to the top of your head and down your forehead and jaw. Come back, come back.

Return to your neck and shoulders and arms and hands. Come back, come back.

Return to your heart and ribs and lungs. Come back, come back.

Return to your will and your pelvic bowl and hips. Come back, come back.

Return to your thighs and knees and calves. Come back, come back.

Return to your ankles and feet. Come back, come back.

Take some time to journal about anything you may have learned from this time. It can help to write things down and return to them in a day or two, as sometimes meanings can unfold in the distance beyond an experience like this.

Exercise: Deeply Listening with the Senses

One thing I notice with working with godds is the tendency to project onto godds what is needed and how you can help. While this is not ill-intentioned, it can be short-sighted. I think of working with godds as any relationship. We need to foster trust with each other, we need to get to know each other, and we need to understand each other to act in our best interests.

Akin to a first date, meeting Gaia can help you understand Her more, and it can help you better understand what your relationship might look like in the future. But another practice that will be helpful is the practice of deep listening. This is something that you can do anywhere, anytime. It doesn't take special props, and it doesn't require any special skills outside of being able to listen in some way. (I say some way because this practice could look slightly different for those without hearing or sight. I hope to offer something for you too.)

I encourage you to travel to nature in some way. This might be stepping outside in your backyard, or it could be traveling to a local park. If you cannot leave your location, turning on a nature show or looking at a nature-inspired picture will work too.

However, you can and will, allow yourself to be immersed in nature. You can use your senses to do this – and use as many as you have access to. You might begin by looking around at the place you are to see what you see. The colors. The shapes. The gradient of light. What can you notice when you use your eyes to experience a place in nature?

Moving to your ears and sound. You might close your eyes to focus or you might simply draw in your breath to become still. Try to listen to things that are close to you. Maybe that's your breath. Perhaps it's an earring that moves when you turn your head. Once you can hear things near you, try to expand your awareness to things that are a little farther away. This might be an animal or a tree branch. Continue to move your awareness out until you can't quite distinguish things that are further in the distance.

Notice next the things you can touch and feel. You might reach out to a plant or to the ground. What does it feel like? What can you notice when you touch nature? What does the wind on your skin feel like? What is the temperature, and how does it change?

You might think about the scents in the air. What can you smell? Do you smell things in the air or do you need to get close to objects to find out what they smell like? If you can't smell anything, can you smell your skin? Can you notice any scent of lingering food on your fingers?

Finally, you can see what you taste in your mouth. This can look like opening your mouth to the air to see if you notice anything new. You could also taste plants that you know to be safe. Or you can make foods from nature and taste what you create.

You can listen deeply to the world as it unfolds around you in all of these moments. It can be so tricky to slow down enough to know this beautiful earth. It is easy to stay on screens and watch videos about things versus being in the real world. Though there might be times when this is safer and easier, I encourage you to continue to find ways to connect with nature to get to know what She might need from you. From us.

Chapter 2

Myths & Stories of Gaia

To Gaia (Gaea, Earth) the Mother of All. I will sing of well-founded Gaia (Earth), mother of all, eldest of all beings. She feeds all the creatures that are in the worlds, all that go upon the goodly land, and all that are in the paths of the seas, and all that fly: all these are fed of her store. Through you, O queen, men are blessed in their children and blessed in their harvests, and to you it belongs to give means of life to mortal men and to take it away. Happy is the man whom you delight to honour! He has all things abundantly: his fruitful land is laden with corn, his pastures are covered with cattle, and his house is filled with good things. Such men rule orderly in their cities of fair women: great riches and wealth follow them: their sons exult with everfresh delight, and their daughters in flower-laden bands play and skip merrily over the soft flowers of the field. Thus is it with those whom you honour O holy goddess (semne thea), bountiful spirit (aphthone daimon). Hail, Mother of the gods (theon mater), wife of starry Ouranos (Uranus, Heaven); freely bestow upon me for this my song substance that cheers the heart!

Translated by Hugh G. Evelyn-White[5] *Homeric Hymn XXX*

One of the best ways to get to know a deity and form a relationship with them is to learn their stories. And when I can find stories that allow for complexity and some recognition of my humanity, all the better for my intrigue. Story is how humans make sense of the world around them, and it is no wonder that Gaia has a few stories in which She arrives as a bit of an instigator. I imagine you can't create a world and not be a little attached to how things turn out.

The Birth of the Cosmos

Verily at first Khaos (Chaos, the Chasm) [Air] came to be, but next wide-bosomed Gaia (Gaea, the Earth), the ever-sure foundation of all the deathless ones who hold the peaks of snowy Olympos, and dim Tartaros (Tartarus, the Pit) in the depth of the wide-pathed Earth, and Eros (Love), fairest among the deathless gods, who unnerves the limbs and overcomes the mind and wise counsels of all gods and all men within them.

From Khaos (Chaos, the Chasm) came forth Erebos (Erebus, Darkness) and black Nyx (Night); but of Nyx (Night) were born Aither (Aether, Light) and Hemera (Day), whom she conceived and bore from union in love with Erebos.

And Gaia (Gaea, the Earth) first bore starry Ouranos (Uranus, the Heavens), equal to herself, to cover her on every side. And she brought forth long Ourea (Mountains), graceful haunts of the goddess Nymphai (Nymphs) who dwell amongst the glens of the mountains. She bare also the fruitless deep with his raging swell, Pontos (Pontus, the Sea), without sweet union of love.

But afterwards she lay with Ouranos (Uranus) and bare [the Titanes (Titans)] deep-swirling Okeanos (Oceanus) [the earth-encircling river], Koios (Coeus) and Krios (Crius) and Hyperion and Iapetos (Iapetus), Theia and Rheia, Themis and Mnemosyne and gold-crowned Phoibe (Phoebe) and lovely Tethys. After them was born Kronos (Cronus), the wily, youngest and most terrible of her children, and he hated his lusty sire.

Translated by Hugh G. Evelyn-White, *Hesiod, Theogony 116 ff*

This is a familiar and unusual creation story to offer for Gaia. She is the creation story, the one who enables history to have a starting point and for Her to have a son and a husband at once – someone who is equal to herself. She is the creatrix, which allows Her to be a mother to all of the world. To me, this story offers a wise and wondrous beginning and a better understanding of the expanse of Her reach today.

The movement from Chaos to the creation of the godds is an integral part of Gaia's stories. This also connects the possibility that we are just as divine. While it was later when Prometheus created humans, we are made from the godds and thus are likely imparted with many of their qualities – and frailties.

This also speaks to the very real idea that we are also responsible for each other, as we are of each other. Connections can lead to responsibilities, I think.

The Castration of Uranus

And Gaia (Gaea, Earth) first bare starry Ouranos (Uranus, Heaven), equal to herself, to cover her on every side, and to be an ever-sure abiding-place for the blessed gods . . . But afterwards she [Gaia] lay with Ouranos and bare [the Titanes (Titans)] deep-swirling Okeanos (Oceanus), Koios (Coeus) and Krios (Crius) and Hyperion and Iapetos (Iapetus), Theia and Rheia, Themis and Mnemosyne and gold-crowned Phoibe (Phoebe) and lovely Tethys. After them was born Kronos (Cronus) the wily, youngest and most terrible of her children, and he hated his lusty sire. And again, she bare the Kyklopes (Cyclopes), overbearing in spirit, Brontes, and Steropes and stubborn-hearted Arges.

And again, three other sons [the Hekatonkheires (Hecatoncheires)] were born of Gaia and Ouranos, great and doughty beyond telling, Kottos (Cottus) and Briareos (Briareus) and Gyes. From their shoulders sprang a hundred arms, not to be approached, and each had fifty heads upon his shoulders on their strong limbs, and irresistible was the stubborn strength that was in their great forms. For of all the children that were born of Gaia and Ouranos, these were the most terrible, and they were hated by their own father from the first. And he used to hide them all away in a secret place of Gaia so soon as each was born, and would not suffer them to come up into the light: and Ouranos rejoiced in his evil doing.

But vast Gaia (Earth) groaned within, being straitened, and she made the element of grey flint and shaped a great sickle, and told her plan to her dear sons. And she spoke, cheering them, while she was vexed in her dear heart: 'My children, gotten of a sinful father, if you will obey me, we should punish the vile outrage of your father; for he first thought of doing shameful things.'

So she said; but fear seized them all, and none of them uttered a word. But great Kronos the wily took courage and answered his dear mother: 'Mother, I will undertake to do this deed, for I reverence not our father of evil name, for he first thought of doing shameful things.'

So he said: and vast Gaia rejoiced greatly in spirit, and set and hid him in an ambush, and put in his hands a jagged sickle, and revealed to him the whole plot. And Ouranos came, bringing on night and longing for love, and he lay about Gaia spreading himself full upon her. Then the son from his ambush stretched forth his left hand and in his right took the great long sickle with jagged teeth, and swiftly lopped off his own father's members and cast them away to fall behind him.

And not vainly did they fall from his hand; for all the bloody drops that gushed forth Gaia received, and as the seasons moved round she bare the strong Erinyes (Furies) and the great Gigantes (Giants) with gleaming armour, holding long spears in their hands and the Nymphai (Nymphs) whom they call Meliai (Meliae) [honey- or ash-tree nymphs] all over the boundless earth.

Translated by Hugh G. Evelyn-White, *Hesiod, Theogony 126 ff,*

Gaia birthed and birthed children with Uranus, eventually birthing what Uranus saw as a horrible beast – the Hekatonkheires. Whether it was from shame, fear, or both, Uranus hid these children from the world so no one would look upon them.

As a mother, Gaia was clear that this action would not go unpunished. She tried to talk these sons into helping her dismember their father, but they froze in fear. Kronos, instead, took up the rounded sickle and snuck into the bedroom of Gaia and Uranus, cutting off his father's genitals in revenge for his shame.

One has to also consider if Gaia was tired of having more children, though She went on to have other beings with other partners.

The War of the Titans

[Kronos (Cronus)] learned from Gaia (Gaea, Earth) and starry Ouranos (Uranus, Heaven) that he was destined to be overcome by his son, strong though he was, through the contriving of great Zeus. Therefore he kept no blind outlook, but watched and swallowed down his children: and unceasing grief seized Rhea. But when she was about to bear Zeus, the father of gods and men, then she besought her own dear parents, Gaia and starry Ouranos, to devise some plan with her that the birth of her dear child might be concealed, and that retribution might overtake great, crafty Kronos for his own father and also for the children whom he had swallowed down. And they readily heard and obeyed their dear daughter, and told her all that was destined to happen touching Kronos the king and his stout-hearted son. So they sent her to Lyetos (Lyettus), to the rich land of Krete (Crete), when she was ready to bear great Zeus, the youngest of her children. Him did vast Gaia (Earth) receive from Rhea in wide Krete to nourish and to bring up. Thither came Gaia carrying him swiftly through the black night to Lyktos first, and took him in her arms and hid him in a remote cave beneath the secret places of the holy earth on thick-wooded Mount Aigaion (Aegaeum); but to the mightily ruling son of Ouranos, the earlier king of the gods, she gave a great stone wrapped in swaddling clothes. Then he took it in his hands and thrust it down into his belly.... After that, the strength

and glorious limbs of the prince increased quickly, and as the years rolled on, great Kronos the wily was beguiled by the deep suggestions of Gaia, and brought up again his offspring... And he set free from their deadly bonds the brothers of his father [Kyklopes (Cyclopes)], sons of Ouranos whom his father in his foolishness had bound. And they remembered to be grateful to him for his kindness, and gave him thunder and the glowing thunderbolt and lightening: for before that, huge Gaia had hidden these.

Translated by Hugh G. Evelyn-White, *Hesiod, Theogony 462 ff*

Gaia revealed to Kronos that his son would overtake him, which caused Kronos to be ever vigilant. In this vigilance, he continued to swallow his children to ensure this would not happen. But Kronos' wife, Rhea, grieved at the many losses. Rhea went to Gaia for help to hide her child from the fate of others. Gaia helped Rhea birth the fated son, Zeus, in another land.

According to Graves, Gaia then took Zeus away to be cared for by nymphs and grew to manhood away from his father before being brought back during the War of the Titans (Graves 40).

Here we see Gaia as someone who can see into the future and passes on those messages. Like many Greek stories, it seems that some complicated things could be cleared up with better communication or a more comprehensive understanding of how fate works.

The Snaring of Persephone

The narcissus, which Gaia (Earth) made to grow at the will of Zeus and to please the Host of Many [Hades] to be a snare for the bloom-like girl [Persephone]–a marvellous, radiant flower. It was a thing of awe whether for deathless gods or mortal men to see: from its root grew a hundred blooms and it smelled most sweetly, so that wide Ouranos (Uranus, Heaven) above and Gaia (Earth) and Thalassa's (Sea) salt swell laughed for joy. And the girl was amazed and reached out with both hands to take the lovely toy: but the wide-pathed earth yawned there in the plain of Nysa, and the lord, Host of Many, with his immortal horses sprang out upon her.

Translated by Hugh G. Evelyn-White, *Homeric Hymn 2 to Demeter 5 ff*

While there are other interpretations of the stories of Persephone and Hades, this snippet speaks to the role of Gaia in making an irresistible narcissus for the young Persephone to find. Again, Zeus seems to be instrumental in this happening. And one has to wonder what Gaia felt about creating a flower that would lead to the events that happened next – the journey of Persephone to the Underworld (whether by force or calling).

I tend to believe Gaia, of course, knew Her role in this story but also was wise enough to understand the context and the wide arc of time. When Persephone is lost from Demeter, the grieving mother puts all of the lands into winter and death. But the agreement of Persephone's return in the Spring leads to the return of the glory of Earth. One might even say the triumph of Earth – and for Gaia.

Exploring Stories of Gaia

While there are stories and myths, I think the stories of Gaia are also found and better understood in the various cycles of Earth. When we can see what is happening in and on Gaia, it can help to better relate and connect – and to see the interdependence that exists and is required.

Gaia is the being of life, death, and renewal. She is not just the blooming and the bounty. She is the holder of the last reach of leaf to sky.

Rocks

There are several types of rocks: igneous (formed by molten material that cools and hardens at the surface of Earth), sedimentary (made of particles of broken rocks), metamorphic (rocks that change due to pressure or heat), and plutonic (made of molten material that cooled beneath Earth's surface). The rocks go through a cycle of creation through the collection of materials, hardening via pressure, movement, chemicals, temperature, wind, water, gravity, etc. Over time, they can break down, erode, and then become the 'ingredients' for a new rock to form. These cycles of formation and degradation can happen over centuries.

Gaia is constantly creating and breaking things down, allowing for rocks that become materials for building or large canyons and mesas that have been worn away by wind and time.

Water

Gaia also exists as the water always present on Earth in various states: solid, liquid, and gas. Water moves from solid ice to a liquid state due to increased temperature and back again due to cooler temperatures to form ice. With more heat, the liquid can become a gas to evaporate and linger in the air as a cloud, fog, or humidity. When the water droplets are too dense, they can fall as rain or arrive as condensation.

Water is a part of all living things. We breathe in water/moisture and we exhale water/moisture. We need to drink water to stay hydrated and expel water when we urinate and sweat. Water is a part of weather patterns, including snow, rain, fog, etc.

Nutrients

As essential to life as water is, so are the building blocks of nutrients – carbon, nitrogen, and oxygen. These are the foundation of nutrients and the raw materials for energy. We take in oxygen when we breathe and we exhale carbon dioxide. This process fuels not only us but also plant life that needs carbon dioxide for their lives. The carbon for plants arrives during photosynthesis which takes sunlight and converts it into energy for plants.

Carbon is in the respiration process and in carbon dioxide released during the decomposition and breakdown of organic materials. Carbon also shows up in water to form bicarbonates.

Nitrogen is the most available molecule on Earth and is essential for amino acids and proteins. It is readily available in the environment.

Natural Processes

While indigenous cultures understand natural processes, it can be challenging to remember that Earth is a dynamic place. It is not a place that can be easily tamed by the wants of humanity. There is a significant impact that humans have on the world and on its processes. But Earth has systems in place to help restore balance when needed. This can look like wildfires to renew forests, diseases or predators to control populations, and new weather patterns to respond to rising land and water temperatures.

While all of this can sound like a school lesson, it is valuable to remember that humans are a part of the process on Earth. Even though we don't think about how photosynthesis works each day, keeping it in mind will remind us of the part we play in the support (or destruction) of Earth. If we want to be more attentive to the needs of Gaia, we can look to Her cycles. We can see what is happening and notice when it changes.

Practice: Notice the Cycles

To encounter Gaia and Her movement in your life, I encourage you to track Her cycles. You can use anything, a pad of paper or a particular journal, to document what Earth is like where you live during a year. You might choose to write down things like:

- The temperatures (high/low)
- The weather pattern
- The barometric pressure
- The humidity
- The moon phase
- The precipitation (rain, snow, hail, etc.)
- Any strange weather occurrences
- Plant behavior – e.g., the plant that had buds in a month when they usually do not

Doing this lets you get a sense of what the year can look like and then compare your notes to the previous years. It can help you begin not only to see the cycles but also begin to live with them. You might know there are certain times of the year when you feel more energized. Or you might learn to plant your flowers earlier because the temperatures are warmer earlier.

All of this helps to live in a relationship with Gaia. She has been telling you about herself each day. But you may not have noticed.

And you can be as creative as you like with this practice. I've seen people knit or weave colors to show weather patterns, creating a piece you can look at and treasure year after year. Or you could take a picture of a particular spot each day at the same time and position. What does it look like in a month? In a day? In a year?

Practice: Tell the Story of Gaia

When I think of the beauty of Gaia and Earth, I sometimes think about how children's stories are so great at tapping into the wonder of the world. If you have been taking time to look at the way the world changes around you, perhaps you can tell the story of Earth as you experience it.

Maybe you and your children or some friends can sit down and draw pictures of the world. Then tell stories about the pictures. Or sit around a table from time to time with pictures of places you have been, telling the story of them. You could even go as far as to find out how the certain places you visited were formed. For example, if you went to the Grand Canyon, you could share pictures and find out how that was created. (Hint: it took a really long time.)

Chapter 3

The Gaia Hypothesis

> *Knowing that you love the earth changes you, activates you to defend and protect and celebrate. But when you feel that the earth loves you in return, that feeling transforms the relationship from a one-way street into a sacred bond.*
>
> Robin Wall Kimmerer, *Braiding Sweetgrass: Indigenous Wisdom, Scientific Knowledge and the Teachings of Plants*

Each day, our lives intersect with the lives of other living beings. Most of the time, we don't remember this. We often discard these thoughts and focus on the things that seem to matter more: the text you just got, the email that needs a carefully worded reply, the bill that appears to be due today.

We move in our world, often in the momentum of the individual. Much of the Western world focuses on the idea that we are separate, that our needs are the most important, and that the earth is the source of industry and energy. (I imagine if you're reading this book, you might think a little differently.)

In the 1970s, James Lovelock, a chemist, and Lynn Margulis, a microbiologist, came up with something different: The Gaia Hypothesis. Also known as the Gaia theory, paradigm, or principle, this proposes that we are not separate from the environment in which we live.

Instead, we are continuously in a relationship with it, helping to regulate each other and to provide each other with the support we need across living organisms and inorganic surroundings.

We are Gaia and Gaia is us.

The History

The Gaia Hypothesis originally stated that:

> *[L]ife, through its interactions with the Earth's crust, oceans, and atmosphere, produced a stabilising effect on conditions on the surface of the planet – in particular the composition of the atmosphere and the climate. With such a self-regulating process in place, life has been able to survive under conditions which would have wiped it out on non-regulating planets.*[6]

If we stop to look at what Earth is made of, we can see how this proposal formed too. After all, Earth, over its many millions of years, created new rocks that produced oxygen, impacting the amounts of carbon, nitrogen, and phosphorus in the environment. All of these atoms are essential for creating and sustaining life.

Lovelock has been quoted as talking about this process of creation and renewal as being the song of life.[7] And his hypothesis seems to speak of the ways in which Earth is a special planet that doesn't act like any other planet in how it sustains life. However, the humans supported by this dynamic regulation are also the ones causing the balance to be upset.

The Gaia Hypothesis showed that while Darwin was right that humans would evolve in their environment, Lovelock brought in the idea that the environment will also change in response to life. This creates a more interactive conversation – and connection.

There is something hopeful in the idea that Gaia looks out for us as we look out for Her. That we are in a constant state of adjusting and shifting to meet the new turns in the road. Lovelock is a complicated human (and who isn't?), but his ideas continue to offer influence and inspiration.

Impact of the Gaia Hypothesis

While there are ongoing conversions about how the Gaia Hypothesis skips a few steps along the road of evolution and the world's creation, it has continued to be discussed and even led to a greater understanding of current ecology.

According to a study published by Oxford Brookes University:

> *The Gaia theory also predicted the causal link between increased biodiversity and increasing stability of populations. The Gaian influence on the development of Evolutionary theory can be found in the idea that life on earth works with the abiotic environment as a self-regulatory system.*[8]

What I find interesting is that arguments against the hypothesis seem to focus on the only way being an all-for-one-and-one-for-all approach. There does not seem to be a place for cooperation or love or doing things for the good of the whole. While it might be challenging for some to see this in the natural world, there are examples everywhere.

Humans have these qualities in many instances. Just because some can't understand how to measure altruism in a plant doesn't mean it doesn't happen. I would offer that we can see this hypothesis in the movement and organization and cooperation of mycelium. Diverse systems exist and co-exist to support each other. There are no wars between fungi, from what I can tell.

The hypothesis has shifted with more information and scientific growth, which is understandable.

The Future of the Gaia Hypothesis

Since the notoriety of this hypothesis in the 1970s, Lovelock has gone on to write about how the takeover of artificial intelligence might be the redemption of Gaia.

> *Gaia might, after all, be saved — by the singularity. This artificial-intelligence takeover, which so alarms many doomsayers, will be our redemption. Lovelock argues that increasingly self-engineering cyborgs with massive intellectual prowess and a telepathically shared consciousness will recognize that they, like organisms, are prey to climate change. They will understand that the planetary thermostat, the control system, is Gaia herself; and, in tandem with her, they will save the sum of remaining living tissue and themselves.*[9]

I too am curious what it would be like if the world (or a lot of it) would consider that we are just as much a part of a cycle and a song with nature as nature is with us. What if we could find the best ways to 'sing' back? What if we could listen deeply and understand the best ways to restore balance?

At the same time, I recognize this might be something that is many generations from now. I am also willing and able to see the possibility that Gaia is more than happy to take care of herself. This might not be what humans would like to see, but Earth will survive. She already has for many billions of years.

Chapter 4

Moving from Myth to Present Day

Gaia
mother of all
foundation of all
the oldest one

I shall sing to the Earth

She feeds everything
that is in the world

Whoever you are
whether you live upon her sacred ground
or whether you live along the paths of the sea
you that fly

it is she
who nourishes you
from her treasure-store

Queen of Earth
through you

beautiful children
beautiful harvests
come

The giving of life
and the taking of life

both are yours

Happy is the man you honour
the one who has this
has everything

His fields thicken with ripe corn
his cattle grow heavy in the pastures
his house brims over with good things

These are the men who are masters of their city
the laws are just, the women are fair
happiness and fortune richly follow them

Their sons delight
in the ecstasy of youth

Their daughters play
they dance among the flowers
skipping in and out

they dance on the grass
over soft flowers

Holy goddess, you
honoured them
ever-flowing spirit

Farewell
mother of the gods
bride of Heaven
sparkling with stars

For my song, life

allow me
loved of the heart

Now
and in my other songs
I shall remember you
Translated by Jules Cashford in *Harvest,* 1988

With the delight (and horror) of myths and expansion of understanding that comes from the Gaia Hypothesis, we enter into the world as we know it: wondrous and in danger. Because of us humans. Because of our impact. Because of disconnection, consumerism, capitalism, and structures of oppression. That certainly brings you back into the present day, doesn't it?

If there's anything I have learned in my activism, you need to start with the truth before you can know what to do next. Having a clear picture of the challenges before you and dismantling outdated thinking will prepare you well.

To be clear, this is a lifelong process of unpacking my beliefs and learning from others who have been doing this work for far longer. But the result is well worth it. It is courageous and it is the promise to our descendants.

I did not grow up in relationship to Earth. I did live in a home with a backyard garden and an understanding that things grew and we could eat them. But I also grew up with processed foods and playtime on concrete. From the time I was little, it wasn't that nature wasn't important, but rather that it was not something that was an everyday experience.

I can imagine I am not the only one with this history. Instead, as an adult, I learned to wander more and to get into the wild places. I learned to travel to ecologies that were unlike the swamps of the Midwest. I went to the Grand Canyon numerous times, absolutely entranced by the idea of a 'ditch' so big that it felt as though it was swallowing me whole when I looked over the edge.

I learned about the wonder of how the earth could smell different in Australia or in the middle of Avebury. And even saying this, I realize the privilege that comes with having the time and resources to visit places beyond where I live now. I wonder how we can create those connections with beauty and wonder within our own little private places. I am certain we can.

Gaia is everywhere. Not just in the dramatic landscapes and the postcards.

The Reality of Climate Change

To care more, we need to know what is happening. It is clear that the damage to the earth is done by large corporations who benefit from producing more, which creates more pollution and harm. This has been proven and cited in multiple studies.

One report showed through self-reported numbers that the top 15 U.S. food and beverage companies generate nearly 630 million metric tons of greenhouse gases every year.[10] When you hear and see things like this, it seems surmountable and useless to be a human that wants to make a change.

And to be fair, climate change isn't coming. It's already here.

- Earth's temperature is rising.
- Weather patterns are becoming more volatile.
- More than one million species are at risk of extinction due to climate change.[11]
- Microplastics are being found in water supplies and animals.[12]
- Data from NASA's Gravity Recovery and Climate Experiment show Greenland lost an average of 279 billion tons of ice per year between 1993 and 2019, while Antarctica lost about 148 billion tons of ice per year.[13]

We are already stepping into a world that is changing because of the impact of humans. The shift will cause humans to need to live in new ways and things will not always be comfortable.

I bring this up to remember that this is happening to Gaia, to Mother Earth. I bring this up because this is devastating.

Moving toward Modern Gaia Worship

While my lens is informed by my work as a Witch, a relationship with Gaia does not have to include magick or spellwork. I imagine that, for some, the idea of worshipping Gaia or focusing in the direction of a mythical being might be odd. But I want to offer something that can be helpful.

Throughout this book, I offer references to the idea that relationship is everything when it comes to supporting Earth. Since so many of us are living on land with a complicated history (read: stolen), there are ways in which we might not feel connected to the earth below our feet. We might talk about it in a sanitized and appropriate way, but it's tricky when it comes to a deeper relationship.

But what if we looked at Earth as a friend? What if we looked to Earth as a being trying to tell us how to be in a better relationship with Her? This is where the idea of Gaia comes in (or could). When we can bring Earth into a form or a relatable energy, it can make more sense of our interactions. When it's Mother Earth or Gaia, we can look to Her and see Her suffering versus a general malaise.

When we lean into anthropomorphism (ascribing human characteristics to nonhuman things[14]), we might see the destruction of a being versus a vague idea. And this isn't a strange concept when you consider how we ascribe human features to our pets. We think they are upset with us because it's how we would react in a situation.

I invite the possibility that we can connect more easily to Earth and to Gaia than we might think. But it will take some imagination.

Gaianism

Formed in response to the Gaia Hypothesis, Gaians work to reduce their impact on the world to support Earth. Those who might call themselves Gaians believe they are a part of the broader experience of organisms on the planet. Humans are all parts of the superorganism of Gaia and are interconnected in that experience. By interacting with awareness, not only does this help support Earth, but it can also promote peace.

Those in Gaianism seek to create balance among living things, including plants, animals, and humans. By grounding themselves in respect for Earth, this practice can become a spiritual understanding of Gaia, without a need for religious tenets.

Reclaiming Witchcraft

> *Because everything is interdependent, there are no simple, single causes and effects. Every action creates not just an equal and opposite reaction, but a web of reverberating consequences.*
>
> Starhawk, *The Earth Path: Grounding Your Spirit in the Rhythms of Nature*

Since the 1970s, Reclaiming Witchcraft has been a tradition focused on activism, including environmental activism. From a *Principles of Unity* that outlines the shared belief in supporting Earth, to a history of protests and actions, this tradition continuously seeks ways to act on devotion to Earth.

It is often said that Reclaiming is an eco-feminist tradition that seeks to unify spirit and politics. By recognizing not only our connections to each other, but also to the earth, we realize our responsibility.

There are many ways to support Gaia through the work of community and magick. In co-created rituals, people can come together to support specific causes or concerns, fueling the intention with energy, drumming, song, dance, and fierce devotion. These rituals might be open to the public or not, they might be planned in the moment or ahead of time.

The Spiral Dance, for example, is an annual ritual focused on earth healing and restoration, happening around the time of Samhain in the northern hemisphere.

The intentions are often centered on healing and transformation, focusing on the present needs of the world (at least as can be encompassed in a few sentences).

- 2021 – With wisdom of the ancestors and love for the descendants, we raise our voices for justice, healing, and peace!
- 2020 – In the midst of uncertainty and the unknown, we come together to call forth the rains of justice and renewal.
- 2019 – To reclaim the golden thread of magic that spans time and draw from the lessons of the past to weave a just and vibrant future.
- 2018 – Where land meets water, together with our beloved dead, we stir a cauldron of tears and outrage to brew an elixir of radical peace and justice.
- 2017 – Riding the knife's edge of history, we face the great challenge of this present moment; to step off the old path and weave futures of strength and joy with the dead and the generations to come.

The music from this ritual (first celebrated in 1979) speaks of how the magick will renew the earth and bring healing to all of the lands, waters, and peoples. With each new ritual, the power of community comes together, dances the spiral of hundreds of people, and sends that energy off into the world to go where it needs to go.

The Spiral Dance Ritual is planned over the year, with input from communities around the globe, with visionings that happen online, and with more online access than in previous years. After all, it's not that earth-friendly to travel to the actual site of the event, nor is it accessible for many reasons.

Though there are certainly ways in which the technology can impact Earth, the streamlining of the ritual also allows for more power to be infused into the spells that support this lovely world in which we get to live.

Earth Day

Because Gaia is the world, and not just our part of the world, let's turn to Earth Day as a way to bring global communities together too. Though having just one day for earth reverence seems little underwhelming, it is also a way to focus energy and bring attention to the many ways in which you can support the environment every day.

Earth Day was first held on April 22, 1970, as a response to the proposal by John McConnell, peace activist, to honor the earth. He wanted to hold it on March 21, since that was the Spring Equinox, but Senator Gaylord Nelson (United States) proposed the eventual date. The Senator hired a young activist (Denis Hayes) to coordinate the event, which ended up being a gathering of more than 20 million people. This has been noted as the largest single-day protest in human history (at that time).[15]

While the first Earth Day was focused on the United States, it soon spread globally with Hayes organizing events in 141 other nations. At the time of writing, Earth Day was said to have included more than 100 million people observing the event in the largest online mass mobilization in history, but the Earth Day website says it's an annual event that engages a billion people each year in more than 190 countries.[16]

While there are certainly ways to see Earth Day as so many other holidays – something that is commercialized and consumerized. It can seem like a token day to atone for the sins that keep Earth in a downward spiral. However, it seems fair that its long-standing tradition acts like a call-in for those who want to reignite their commitment to the environment.

There are so many holidays and days of importance that are singular, but their message and spirit are something to remember the entire year. Perhaps Earth Day can do this too.

One might say the creation of Earth Day is a more extensive and more collaborative practice of supporting Gaia, even if it's not called that, nor was that its intention.

Activist Groups

It makes sense to introduce some groups already doing activism for Earth so you too can get involved in your local areas. Before we get started, I recognize that not everyone identifies as an activist. This might be a word that is frightening or overwhelming in response to your own experience and/or the way activists are portrayed in the media.

I want to offer you the permission slip to be the kind of activist you can be. Really, it can be that simple. When your goal is to support Gaia and to support the world around you, it is really up to you what that looks like. While it's true that people will have their own ideas about what things 'should' look like, you are an individual and can only do what you can.

I encourage you to figure out what you are passionate about. When it comes to activism, there are many flavors and many avenues to take. You might not be as passionate about manatees as someone else, but you might be passionate about bees. Think about what you already want to protect and what you already love. This will help you understand what you want to do with your energy.

While I know there might come a time when someone is critical of the way you enact your personal activism, remember: you cannot do everything. You cannot do things the way everyone wants you to. You can give what you can.

As one final note, activism is not a process of perfection. It is a process of learning, unlearning, and acting on what you know at the time. It is typical and expected for you to think one thing and then change your mind. You might do something and get feedback about it. You have the chance to learn from this moment. It might not mean you do anything differently, but when you get feedback, it's because the person wants you to learn from a mistake or misstep. This can also be an opportunity.

Remember, in supporting the earth (or being a witch or human), there are many ways. Find the one that calls to you. Follow that. Do that. When you can go into activism with the idea that you will not be perfect, you will likely be consistent in your efforts. And consistency is what keeps things going.

A few essential tips to get you started would be to:

- Ask what your neighborhood needs.
- Check out events at local parks and water sources.
- Speak to the local council or government about their programs.
- Look into local schools and their events, including universities and colleges.
- Research environmental groups via the internet and find local chapters.

Here is the part where I recommend some environmental groups and organizations to follow and support. I will list the ones I have found to be most diligent in their work, as well as those I have worked with in the past. I have not worked with all of these groups. I researched them and found them listed as being the most effective with their funding and events. (I will list them in alphabetical order to avoid any order of preference. This is also not an inclusive list by any means. Please research and support local organizations first since they tend to need volunteers and funding more than larger non-profits.)

350.org – This global organization is working toward ending fossil fuel usage and bringing renewable energy to the world through a fast and just transition for all. Founded in 2008, this group was named after the safe concentration of carbon dioxide in parts per million: 350.

Earth Day Network – Though we've already covered a little of this group, these are the folks who are organizing Earth Day. They are committed to preserving and protecting health, families, and livelihoods by acting on climate change. Earth Day Network is committed to acting boldly, innovating broadly, and implementing change equitably.

Extinction Rebellion (XR) – Extinction Rebellion is a decentralized, international, and politically non-partisan movement using non-violent direct action and civil disobedience to persuade governments to act justly on the Climate and Ecological Emergency.[17] The group empowers people to form their own XR groups in their local areas to activate change.

Environmental Defense Fund (EDF) – Called one of the world's leading environmental organizations, EDF has been around since 1967, using science to find ways to protect Earth.

Greenpeace – The goals of Greenpeace include protecting biodiversity, preventing pollution and abuse of the ocean, land, air, and freshwater, ending nuclear threats, and promoting peace, global disarmament, and non-violence.

National Resources Defense Council (NRDC) – Since 1970, the NRDC has been focusing on ensuring the rights of all people to clean air, clean water, and healthy communities by partnering with businesses, elected leaders, and community groups to identify priorities.

Rainforest Alliance – This is an international non-profit organization seeking to protect forests, improve the livelihoods of farmers and forest communities, promote their human rights, and help them mitigate and adapt to the climate crisis.[18]

Sierra Club Foundation – By empowering people to protect and improve the environment, the Sierra Club Foundation seeks to solve the climate crisis, secure protections for public land, support projects and programs to educate across economic, cultural, and community groups, and build a more diverse environment.

The Nature Conservancy – This organization is looking toward 2030 as a timeline for solving climate and biodiversity crises, focusing on global warming and conservation efforts. The goals include reducing emissions, protecting and restoring natural habitats, conserving 10 billion acres of ocean, conserving 1.6 billion acres of land, conserving 620,000 miles of rivers, and supporting 45 million local stewards.

World Wildlife Federation (WWF) – WWF is the world's largest conservation organization with more than five million supporters worldwide in 100+ countries supporting 1,300 conservation and environmental projects.

And this is such a small sample of groups. If there is any part of the world you are interested in supporting more than others, you can do an internet search and likely find a related non-profit. For example, if you are committed to ocean projects, you can find groups that only focus there. If you want to save the polar bears, you can find like-minded groups.

The more you can find something you are already concerned about, the more likely you are to engage fully and for the long term. Find what calls to you.

Exercise: What Do I Do?

For this practice, I encourage you to get a piece of paper or a journal, as well as a writing instrument. Set aside time to work on this practice and see where it takes you next.

Set a timer for 10 minutes. Once the timer starts, write down everything you can for this prompt: What does Gaia need? You can list anything and everything that comes to your mind. I encourage you to not put down your pen until the time is up. You want to let your brain help you write, but also let go of making things perfect.

Write and continue to write words, phrases, sentences, etc., even if you need to write the same thing multiple times because you've run out of things to say. Once you've completed the writing sprint, stop and close your eyes. You may need to stretch your wrist too.

When you're ready to open your eyes again, do so and look at the list. Take your pen or pencil and circle everything that jumps out at you. They might be exciting or silly or curious. Maybe circle ten things. Once you circle them, I invite you to craft this into a poem or a small story. You can add other words to help them make sense.

This might become a prayer for Gaia or a To Do list to help care for the world. You can repeat this whenever you feel uninspired or hopeless, as we all do. Recharge your earth-loving heart by asking creativity to lead the way.

Exercise: Let Go of Perfection

One of the things I notice about the practice of Earth worship today is a desire to be a pristine and pure practitioner. Am I a good enough activist? Am I doing enough?

We will get nowhere if we are stuck in perfection. Perfection is a tool of white supremacy. It tells us we are not good enough unless we meet a certain standard or expectation. By dismantling this thought, we can move out of inaction and into progress.

I want you to start by listing out everything you think you are doing wrong in supporting Earth and working with Gaia. Write them all out on paper and don't stop until you genuinely run out of things to write. Be specific and be honest about what you think you are missing right now.

Once you have that list in your hand, I invite you to read it to yourself. What happens when you read this? What does your body feel like? What would it feel like if you were telling these things to a friend? What would it feel like if you told yourself these things daily?

Who told you these things? Who wants you to believe these things? How have your actions been impacted by the way you think about yourself?

On the other side of the paper (or a new piece), I invite you to write down all of the things you want to do for Gaia. What do you want to say about yourself? What do you want to think about yourself? What messages would inspire you and motivate you? What would you like to hear someone say about you? This is the paper you want to go back to when you feel too small or too ineffective. (Those days will come.)

There is no need to be perfect in any activism. But when your self-criticism keeps you from action, that's a good time to stop. Think about what messages you're telling yourself and see if you can change things. Even if you don't believe in the positive messaging at first, the more you can turn your brain in that direction, the more you will see your actions shift too.

Chapter 5

Working Magick with Gaia

Earth, the beautiful, rose up,
Broad-bosomed, she that is the steadfast base
Of all things. And fair Earth first bore
The starry Heaven, equal to herself,
To cover her on all sides and to be
A home forever for the blessed gods.
Edith Hamilton, *Mythology,*

At one point, Hamilton speaks about the children of Gaia and Uranus as monsters (Hamilton 79). They are described as being like humans, but not quite. This is said to be caused by the fact that they were born into a world that didn't exist yet. And as such, they didn't have a context or a place to understand themselves or their roles. They were wild forces and energies without life in existence.

I share this to acknowledge that true connection with Earth, with Gaia, and with the world requires an understanding of our place in it. While you may not know the exactness of your presence, coming to a place where you can understand the interconnectedness of the earth will allow you to know how you can be an agent of change and a helpful supporter.

The practices in this section veer away from talking about what to do and move into the magickal realm. While not all of these practices are necessarily 'magick,' they are designed to help you move beyond the logical mind and into the wisdom of bodies connected to ancestors and descendants. The bodies that are made of Earth's wisdom. Sometimes, we just need other ways to access this wisdom.

Navigating Grief & Despair

In my own journey, I have noticed something often stands in my way of taking action as a human: grief. I have met times when my grief and despair are so large that I am frozen by them. I am taken down by it. I am overcome, and I am unable to think clearly – or to think any of my actions will matter.

Navigating ecological grief and the despair that can come from thinking you have hurt Mother Earth is a necessary step. And it is something you will need to return to again and again. While I'd like to reassure you that Earth will heal easily, quickly, and completely…I can't say that with any confidence or optimism. I think we will meet many more dark times, literally and figuratively. I believe we will find ourselves in strange new situations and uncomfortable worlds. And this is saying it kindly.

Does that mean we should just give up and let go? That is always an option. But for me, I think of the children here and those on the way. Perhaps I will not see the results of my actions in my lifetime, but I believe everything I do will have an impact. This is a great responsibility.

If you find yourself stuck in the chambers of grief, I invite you to return to this work to help your heart.

Place a bowl of clean water in front of you. Close your eyes and come to a place of stillness. Take a moment to breathe and relax until you are in the present moment, where everything is just as it is. You are not hurting or helping. You are in between.

In that safe moment, pull up a movie screen in your mind. This can be a literal screen or it could just be the impression of one. Only you know how your mind works. Pull this screen up and allow it to show you what worries you most about the world. Maybe it is the destruction of rainforests. Perhaps it is the loss of wildlife. Or the drying up of oceans. Or the sinking of cities.

Whatever you fear, bring it up on the screen. It is on a screen away from you and only a movie of what could be. If there is any moment where you are overcome, you can turn away from the screen and remember to breathe. It can help to put a hand on your heart to activate a calming sensation.

When you experience or see the things happening, allow yourself to feel the grief. Let it rise up in your body, your throat, your mind. This might make certain places in your body tense. You might want to cry. Do whatever it is that you feel is the best way for you. Allow yourself to feel the grief. There is no right or wrong way.

Allow your body to feel deeply into this experience. You don't have to tell yourself why; just feel what you feel. There is no judgment here, only emotions that are real for you. There is no right or wrong way to do this. Allow yourself to follow the feeling as it moves through your body, as you weep, scream, or whatever it is you decide to do.

Without trying to fix yourself, let this run its course. When things feel done or complete enough, I invite you to think of all that grief running out of your body. Drop those feelings and tension into the bowl of water. Or you can use the water to wash the parts of you that need some refreshment. Allow yourself to release that grief. To loosen its hold on you. To allow it to be both present and unstuck from you.

Wash your head, hands, heart, and whatever else needs it. Allow the grief to flow away from the present. Offer a prayer to the person holding this grief, thanking them for their love. Offer a blessing to the person who will have grief again in the future, reminding them that they can let go when they need to.

Open your eyes and return to your place when you feel ready.

It is wise to allow grief to move through you. This is not an exercise of exorcising your grief, but rather allowing it to inform you. When you make space for grief, it does not get stuck or get in the way of what you want to do next. It also becomes familiar so you can feel it every day if needed. It becomes less of an enemy and more of a companion. With great love comes grief, grief because all that we love will someday leave us. Absolutely everything we love will no longer be there one day. And we will grieve. It is wise to learn to do this now. To do this regularly. To allow it to remind us of our deep love, which also gives us courage and strength to continue.

Oracular Work

Joanna Macy's work is one of the resources I have been exposed to in working with Gaia, Mother Earth, the environment, etc. Her writing informs my practices and thinking, so I want to share some of how her work has helped me. And hopefully, it will help you too.

You can do a practice with a group of people called the Council of All Beings.[19] I suggest you have at least five people for this work, and it will work best with a group that is committed to supporting the work of environmental activism (however that shows up for you).

This is an exercise that will help you get a better understanding of what Earth might be asking of us right now, based on how Earth speaks through us right now.

Before I explain how I learned this practice, it is important to recognize this working is cited as originally being invented by Joanna and John Seed in 1985 when they were leading workshops in Australia. The two connected and wanted to create an exercise that decentralized the human-led thinking often arising in conversations about Earth.

Here is the way that I would guide the exercise in a group. The group members who wanted to experience the energy of an animal or plant form would volunteer, so we would know who was participating. I would also encourage at least one person to write down things during the exercise. They would not take on the energy of an animal or plant. They would be someone who would stay solidly in their thinking and energy.

Ideally, the plants and animals in the room would be different so there would be diversity. But they can be anyone that the participants are interested in or that the group wants to hear from.

Once these have been chosen, there might be space to allow each of those people to spend private time thinking about these energies and to start to feel them as a part of their physical body. It can be helpful too for each person to make a mask of their animal or plant so they can put that on during the exercise.

After a time that feels appropriate (with more preparation time given for the first time this takes place), the people who are to be speaking or animals or plants will sit in chairs in front of those who are witnessing or taking notes. Each being will start by putting on their mask and feeling into that energy they decided to call forward. In turn, they would introduce who they are. For example, "I am tiger and I speak for all tigers."

If I'm guiding this, I will thank them for coming and imparting their wisdom. I will ensure they are comfortable by asking if they need anything more before we begin. I would also ask if it was okay for me to ask them questions. Once I got the agreement, I would move through different questions. You can choose these as you like, but here are some ideas.

- What are the biggest challenges of your species?
- What are the dangers ahead?
- What do you need humans to understand or know?
- What do you want to tell humans?

In Macy's description, she has a human form go in the middle of the animals and plants during the question about what they want humans to know or hear. The human should not respond during this portion. They should continue to listen and to write down anything they might hear for future reference.

This can be a humbling and startling experience for those who are humans. To have the human voice not prioritized is not the norm. But it can help to create a deeper understanding and a more nuanced conversation about actions.

To wrap up this practice, the beings will take off their masks while they impart a gift for the humans. They might say things like, "As Tiger, I offer you the gift of strength and adaptation." Again, all the messages are written down and reviewed when the exercise is over.

As you can see, this can be a powerful experience. If you are a group that regularly works in magickal circles, it can help to create a strong container before you begin. You might want to cast a circle, call in elements, and call in other allies to support this work.

You can also create any format you like, depending on the group's needs. I recommend that the first time you do this sort of work, you keep a time container so you can stay on track. When you are more comfortable with this working, you can agree to a longer period of time.

A few things to keep in mind:

- It helps to have a guide to move through the steps of the process. This person will know what questions to ask, and they will make sure the beings are respected along the way. They are to be gracious and grateful. They are to ask permission to move on and to be certain to make sure each being has said everything they need to say before moving to another question.
- Also, it is wise to be well nourished and hydrated before this process. You want to keep your full attention and presence during this working.
- I would also encourage you to have some sort of food or drink ready when the masks are taken off, the circle

is opened, and the exercise is done. You want to ground before you start to read what has been shared.

- Some might want to share the wisdom right away, while others might want to let it rest and come back to it the next day. That is a choice that is up to you.
- Finally, I would encourage the ones who were beings during this exercise to track any thoughts or dreams that come up later. There might be more wisdom that is waiting for them. But there is also a slight warning to be clear about what is the human talking versus the being.

Ideally, the beings would be completely gone from the humans when the masks are removed. This is something that can be said and agreed to ahead of time. The masks should be covered and moved to another location to 'rest.'

I encourage this exercise when a group is unclear in their direction when working on environmental causes. The confusion often comes from being too invested in human logic versus remembering the animals and the plants.

Work with the Dead

Environmental activists are murdered[20] more frequently than you realize. Those who are working to protect the earth die by suicide. And others will die because they come to the natural end of their lives, even if it is earlier than we'd hope. While this sounds dire and depressing, I encourage you to stay with me for a minute. Just as we can step into the energies of animals and plants, we can also call to the energy of those who came before.

Many pagans will celebrate Samhain, or Halloween, as a time to remember ancestors. Some might call them Beloved Dead or Mighty Dead. Some beings may not be alive on this plane anymore, but they are undoubtedly present for those who might want to call to them. They have wisdom and perspective that we don't have in this current time. And by working with the dead, we can create a connection that informs and heals.

One of the most common practices of working with the dead is to create an altar and leave offerings for them. You might begin with an altar of pictures of those who have died, even if you didn't know them. You can create an altar meant to hold the spirits of the deceased. This might include things to hold the energy of their causes, e.g., a bowl of water for the oceans, a leaf for the forests, etc. Make a special place for these dead so they know they are remembered.

This altar should be a place you regularly visit, just as you would for any deity or special being. You can leave them an offering of your service or an offering of clean water, a new token of nature, etc. You can talk to them and ask them about the way they would handle a certain problem. You might have a notebook that you leave on the altar, where you write down your questions and ask for answers in dreams. When you receive a response, you can write that down to keep track of that wisdom.

Often people at this point will wonder if this is okay to do. Is it okay to ask the dead for help? I believe there is no harm in asking. And I also believe I have no expectation for the dead. They are also able to say no or to ignore me.

In this instance, I might offer that those working for environmental causes are more likely to help as their work was unfinished. It is wise to make sure you understand their specific causes and find ways to honor them by finishing what they started. Or continuing what they started. This can connect you to their stories and to their energies even more strongly.

I also think it's wise to tell the stories of the dead to keep their memories alive. In my tradition of Reclaiming Witchcraft, we say, "What is remembered, lives." We can continue their legacy by remembering the stories and ways of those who have gone before.

My message to you about working with the dead is to also remember that you are becoming an ancestor every day. How can you live more in alignment with your values and your activism? By living the way you want to live, you are creating a future and a past that will celebrate all ancestors.

Gaia & Rhea & Demeter & More

One of Gaia's many children, born of two parents and some born of just Gaia, was Rhea, who often gets more attention than Gaia. She is often called the Mother of the Gods, even though Gaia is the one who mothered Her. Rhea does not seem to have a large following if we look back in history, though She was the one to hide Zeus from his father.

Some thought that Demeter was the 'replacement' for Gaia after a time. As Demeter was the goddess of harvest and agriculture, which would be very important to the people, it makes sense that She would be worshipped frequently. People needed their crops to grow and for harvests to be plentiful. However, I would not conflate the two, even though they are indeed intertwined.

But I brought these beings together because I think Mother Nature is hard to narrow. And when working with magick for the planet, I imagine calling on multiple deities would be helpful.

In working magick for the planet, here is a way to work with multiple deities simultaneously. The more energy, the better. The more who are connected to the planet the better. You may want to call on all of Gaia's children, monsters or not. (Perhaps especially the monsters for those who might need some reminders of the ferocity of Gaia.)

Common practices to call on the energies of beings include altars, offerings, spells, etc. For this practice, I might encourage a ritual of connection between Gaia, Rhea, and Demeter. All mothers and all connected to the earth. (Please remember that while I use 'She' for mothers, I know that not all mothers use these pronouns.)

Since this book seeks to support the planet, I would encourage you to minimize what you need to buy for a ritual and look instead to what you already have available. If you have things that would work instead of what I suggest, that would be great.

What I suggest:

Flowers
Stones or shells

First, you will want to create some sort of sacred container. I like to cast a circle by starting in the North and moving around to where I began, clockwise. Then I like to bring energy from above to below and envision the sphere around the space I am in. I then would call on each of the goddesses to aid me in my work. Here is something you might use or allow your heart to guide what needs to be said:

Dear Gaia, Mother Earth, Creatrix and Mother of us all. Be with me and aid my work.
Dear Rhea, Mother of Gods, you who birthed Demeter. Be with me and aid my work.
Dear Demeter, Goddess of Harvest and Plenty, you who feed and nourish us. Be with me and aid my work.

From there, I would take the flowers and shells and think about the energy of each of the goddesses. As I think about their gifts and what they have birthed, I would lay flowers and shells in the middle of the circle. As I laid each one down, I would remember what their birthing had brought into my life.

Gaia, you birthed the oceans that I love.
Rhea, you birthed the fertility of my life.

Demeter, you birthed the ability to feed the hungry.

Again, you can let your heart guide you in these offerings. As you do, you can create an altar on the ground, one of beauty and birthing. Allow yourself to sink into the waves of what has come into your life. All of the ways that it can flow forward into the world.

This ritual is one of gratitude for all that has been given and given again. You might offer things in return for what has been given. I encourage you to let this take the time it takes. There is no need to rush or to get through the ritual with these beings.

But once you have named and thanked, I invite you to lay in the altar you have created and remember that you are a gift of these beings too. Allow that to be a moment where you can feel their blessings shower down on you. Enjoy this and take it into your bones and heart.

Once you are filled with the blessings of these beings, take up the altar (whatever it is made of) and thank the energies you have called. Take this altar and place it somewhere of importance in your home, where you can look upon it and remember your place too.

Ethical Foraging

Building a relationship with the land is part of the magick of Gaia. As you have seen and read, She is not one to be trifled with when things feel out of balance. She will respond. She will act accordingly.

In many circles, I see the conversation of foraging[21] as a way to build a better connection with Mother Earth. By harvesting from Her bounty, we receive Her gifts. However, this is veering into a colonizer mindset when not done ethically. Remember, colonizers believe they have the right to anything within their reach – without concern for how it impacts the land or its people. Don't be that person.

To begin, you will want to figure out what the ecology looks like in your part of the world. What plants live around you? How do they live with other plants? When do they grow? How do they grow? Where do they live? How are they supported?

DO NOT harvest anything until you know what it is. Be sure of what you are gathering, even if you're not going to ingest it. Too many plants look similar and can harm you, your pets, or your family.

While you can certainly read about these things in books, I encourage you to first seek out local guides and indigenous folks whenever possible. See if there are local resources that can help you get in touch with the land to better understand how foraging might be helpful – or not. These groups and individuals can also help you with the legalities of foraging in your area.

You are bound to learn that you need to ask for the consent of the plants before you take anything from them. Now is the best time to learn if you're not usually in communication with plants. You want to first sit with the plants you have in your yard or near your home. Sit with them and try to understand what their energy feels like. This might be an exploration that looks like sitting with the plant, touching the plant (if you can), tasting the plant (if you can), and making notes about what you feel when you engage.

Once you can understand what it means to communicate with a plant, you can feel more comfortable asking a plant if it's okay to take from it. And if you are unclear at any time, take that answer as a 'no.'

Other things to keep in mind with ethical foraging:

- Take only what you need – You only want to take what you will use quickly so as not to cut the plant so far back that it can't recover.
- Offer something back – I like the idea of offering something back to the plant, either a hair or water or some other item that shows your reciprocation of their gift to you.

- Be mindful of where you are – If possible, always try to leave the area exactly as you found it without harming any surrounding structures or fauna.

This work can be a great way to build a strong relationship with the local area, allowing you to be more in tune with the growing and dying cycles. This will also help you be aware when things change or when they need additional help. If you move to a new area, start from the beginning to make sure you are creating solid, sustainable partnerships with the plants you visit.

Relationships are meant to be reciprocal. The more you can cultivate this with the natural world, the more likely you will do this in the world of humans too. Give and take. But also give without needing to take or without expecting something in return. Not every trip to forage will offer you what you need. You can still give something back.

Consumerism in a Consumerist World

Before starting this section, I want to confess something: I like stuff. I like shiny new things and I like the way that new things feel in my hands. I am a physical being who likes stuff.

However, as I continue to deepen my relationship with Earth and my connection with Gaia, I understand that consuming is an unending, destructive cycle. Continuing to take and take and take from Earth is not sustainable. It is not helpful. It is in direct opposition to caring for Earth. And... some things need to be bought. There are places where you can't grow your food or have access to things to make clothes, etc.

There is no simple answer because the world is complicated. Not everyone has the same resources and abilities, but I want to bring the idea of minimizing consumption into the conversation. While I am certainly not a purist when it comes to this, it is something I strive to be mindful of because I like Earth and want it to be around for a while.

I offer a few things that will help reduce your consumption.

Find out what you have – For many of us, it's not that we want or even need to buy more; it's that we have so many things that we forget what we have. I encourage you to spend some time taking inventory of what you own right now. What is in those cupboards? What books do you have? What toiletries do you own that you haven't used? This is not a shaming exercise, but an awareness exercise. The more you know about what you have, the more you can make decisions based on what is missing and needed.

Reconsider packaging – Whenever possible, it's wise to stay away from things that are heavily packaged. Though you have little control over this when items are shipped, you can choose things that are not in plastic when you go to the store. Or you can select paper containers or other options. The more you can reduce packaging, refill things, and bring your bags to reuse, the less you will bring in your door. And the less you will throw away.

Challenge yourself – Again, do this as it makes sense to you; it might be fun to try not to buy a particular item over a month. For example, if you notice you buy a lot of clothes, maybe try to have one month where you don't buy anything new. This way, you can use what you already have and find out if you need anything new.

Look to borrow or buy secondhand – Social media might sometimes be a pain, but it also has groups that can help you borrow or buy secondhand. All you need to do is put a post out there with what you want and you'll likely find someone who can help. Libraries often have online catalogs so you can get things for free with your library card, including audiobooks, eBooks, movies, and more. Thrift stores, charity shops, and op shops (or whatever you call secondhand or consignment shops) are also great places to find things you might need without buying something new.

But the real way to step away from consumer thinking is to focus on things outside of buying and procuring.[22] When you notice yourself buying something, stop yourself and ask if you need the item. It sounds simple, but it's a mindfulness practice. More often than not, we buy things because we see others have them or we see them as filling an emotional need. We can reduce consumption if we slow down and ask if we need it.

When we reduce consumption, we will reduce the resources we need to use on the earth. I'm not going to pretend that cutting down on your shopping will solve all the problems. Many people in the world don't think about this – or need a certain level of consumption for survival (e.g., accessibility). However, aligning your actions with your beliefs is a way to live a life alongside Gaia. It is a way to support Mother Earth and to perhaps even encourage others to think about their buying habits.

If you change how you approach your consumerism, your friends will notice. And they might ask why. This offers you the chance to spread the good word of environmental activism, without having to hold up a protest sign.

Making Oaths with and to Gaia

If you find yourself in a collective or a group that is committed to changing the way you show up for Mother Earth, you may want to create a ritual of commitment. There are many ways to do such a ritual, but here is one that can help your group feel committed to your causes and each other. I learned this exercise as an ally circle, but I have modified it for this purpose.

You will need:

An altar to Gaia, simple is fine. Place this off to the side of the main area.

At least five people.

Space to move.

Chairs for those who need to sit at any time.
Someone to say things to move the exercise along.

(Note: This ritual can also be done over a video call,[23] which I will explain at the end. You don't need to be in person.)

First things first, you want to acknowledge Gaia and Her presence. Make some sort of statement that the work you are doing is work that is in service to Her. You are making oaths and promises with Her watching over you.

Start with everyone standing or sitting in a circle. When someone is ready, they will go to the circle's center and make an oath. I promise to ___________. They will stand in the center of the circle and anyone who joins them in this oath will stand next to them. Those who come closer are those who are promising to help the person or they promise the oath themselves. This doesn't have to be shared aloud.

The people in the center will take time to lock eyes of understanding and agreement. If I lead this practice, I will say, "Look around to see who shares this oath with you." And then the people in the center will look at those in the outer circle who are not joining them. "And look to see who supports you." Once everyone has had a good look, I will say, "And now return to the circle."

This practice can repeat for as many rounds as needed. But I will caution that too many rounds can lead to forgetting what you have promised. It can be wise to promise only a few things and make good on those before doing more.

After everyone has had a turn and feels finished, you might wrap it up by thanking Gaia for witnessing your oaths.

This practice online will look like this:

- Everyone has their camera on so faces can be seen.
- Once everyone is ready, everyone turns their camera off.

- Whoever goes first will turn on their camera and speak.
- When you resonate with the speaker, you also turn on your camera to join the inner circle.
- If you do not resonate, you keep your camera off.
- A leader of this exercise can speak and join in as they did before.
- Once all camera-on people are seen and the outside camera-off people are acknowledged as supporting, the cameras all go off again.
- Repeat until done.

This practice can be adjusted for a myriad of purposes, so have fun with it.

A few troubleshooting notes:

- It's best to keep your oath to one sentence. No need to explain yourself unless it's confusing to others and they're not sure they can resonate.
- If you step into the center and no one comes with you, the leader can say something like, "Noticing what it's like to stand in your truth and to witness yourself. And then looking out to see all who support you." While it's not hugely common, this does happen and a wise phrase like this can make it less awkward.
- Let the witnessing be long enough for everyone to make eye contact as possible. Don't rush that part.
- Make sure you promise what you can do.
- It can help to be grounded before and after this practice.

The ally circle reminds us that we are not alone and that others often share our thoughts. In knowing this, we can feel more empowered and supported.

Creating Rituals for Gaia

While we've already created rituals and activities to celebrate and support Gaia, I wanted to offer some guidelines for creating your own. Often, I hear that people feel overwhelmed by the possibilities and having a clear starting point can help. Let's do that now.

Here are tips I would offer for working with Gaia:

Be in nature – When you want to work with or connect with Gaia, why not go outside? Try just feeling Her energy in the sunshine, the forest, the water, and the rain. You don't have to 'do' anything but be with Her. And you can also do a full ritual in the wonders of nature. Take your shoes off and feel the ground. Let the wind take your hair. Feel the difference between sun and shade on a hot day.

Use Her epithets and poetry – If you like words, go back to the poetry or the epithets in this book to read them to Her. You might sit under a tree and read Her poetry, like you might a lover or friend. Write new poems, make up songs, bang on a drum for Her.

Notice Her beauty out loud – One of the best ways to celebrate and work with Gaia is to notice how lovely She is by naming it. You might be talking to a friend or just walking down a road. Let your voice carry your awe and your gratitude. Let nothing go unnoticed.

Notice Her fierceness out loud – And also notice Her fierceness. The way the wind breaks things away. The way the water carries the shore to flatness or ridge. The way the rain pools. Not everything is meant to blossom all the time. Do not shy away from what is true and real and part of the grand cycle of life and death.

Make an offering daily – You live on the earth each day, so why not find a way to offer something each day? You can offer your attention, time, resources, heart, etc. You might create a daily practice of loving the earth as best you can. You might open a window each morning and send your love to the day.

Actions are spells – The more action you can take to support the places that you love, the more you will call in the magick of healing. Actions are cumulative. Consistency is a gracious offering.

Less is more – While you might have grand ideas and want to be in supplication to the earth, remember that devotion is a more powerful prayer. It feels great to lie on the ground, but it also feels wonderful to stretch your arms to the sky. Consume less. Take less. Know what you need and what is available.

Simple is best in this relationship. Kindness and care are the ways to work magick on all consciousness levels.

Chapter 6

Cultivating a Relationship with Gaia

Only when we've truly fallen back in love with the Earth will our actions spring from reverence and the insight of our interconnectedness. Yet many of us have become alienated from the Earth. We are lost, isolated and lonely. We work too hard, our lives are too busy, and we are restless and distracted, losing ourselves in consumption. But the Earth is always there for us, offering us everything we need for our nourishment and healing: the miraculous grain of corn, the refreshing stream, the fragrant forest, the majestic snow-capped mountain peak, and the joyful birdsong at dawn.

Thich Nhat Hanh

In the time I have lived on Earth, I have realized that I am more committed to people, places, and causes with which I have built strong relationships. When I am not spending time and energy to get to know someone, there is little my attention can attach to.

I will feel separateness when I am not in a true relationship. I don't tend to fight for those who are mere acquaintances, after all. But when I can understand their experience or I can emphasize with their troubles, I can take action.

Getting to Know Gaia

I hope that this book has given you some background on what is currently known about Gaia from the source texts, as well as through the eyes of scholars, researchers, poets, and mystical experiences. Like any relationship, I encourage beginning with a strong foundation, as though you were dating this deity versus just studying them. Remember that the earth is not separate from you; you too are the earth. And since I also think we are all divine, Gaia is alongside you, not above or beyond you.

Read Her stories – Find other translations of Her stories and myths to get a sense of who She is and how She is talked about by others. This can help have a broader picture of Her reputation and how it may have shifted depending on the translation and time of translation.

Build an altar – While I imagine you don't build altars for your friends (but maybe?), building an altar to a deity is a great way to create space in your life for this being. You might look for pictures of Gaia that resonate with you or draw one based on your trance experience from Chapter 1. This picture can be the entire altar or you might want to add more things, e.g., offerings of barley and honey. As you continue with your relationship, you might want to add other things that make sense in the context of your individual relationship. For example, you might have flyers for actions and protests. You might have spells and messages to offer to Her.

Sit with Gaia – One of the most important, but often overlooked, ways to connect with a deity is to just be with them. This means sitting at the altar or a place that seems like an excellent place to connect. You sit there and ask them to come to you. And then you wait. This will create space for the deity to see your devotion and consistency. These are building blocks for any good relationship, after all. Show up. Expect nothing. Offer what you can and will.

Do things that support Her – Taking action to help Gaia turns a relationship from a thought experiment into a partnership. You can find local events that support cleaning up a park or other green space. You might look for ways to plant things that attract pollinators or remove a lawn that requires water. Figure out things you can do that are within your means and abilities. That said, I also encourage you to be open to listening to what Gaia might ask of you. She might ask you to go to a certain place and hug a tree or to meet with a person who needs help with their garden. Be willing and open to the possibility that She might have ideas too.

Getting to know Gaia is a process of action and support. I believe that this is a relationship that requires more giving on your part than on Gaia's part. This is a relationship that will ask you to be accountable. It will be a relationship that will continue to ask more of you because Earth is changing, far faster than any of us might realize.

I hope that any level of relationship with Gaia is supportive of you, as well as Her. You don't have to devote every moment of your life to Her – or anyone – but I encourage you to think about how you can become a better partner, ally, accomplice, and co-conspirator with the home in which you live and love.

Temples of Gaia

If Gaia is a being who can inform you of the best steps to support Her and save Her, then I invite the possibility of building temples for Her. This is not to say you need to emulate ancient Greece, but instead I want to encourage you to spread small altars to Her around the spaces you live. She is not just contained in the space you are or the places you visit most frequently.

Natural offerings – A simple way to spread offerings to Gaia and to have places to return to is to leave small offerings in natural spaces. If you live in an urban setting, you can leave small, natural items in corners or windowsills. The main suggestion from me is that you only leave biodegradable things.

Messages – You can write down blessings to Gaia and leave them around natural spaces. Again, use biodegradable paper so it can break down in the weather. You might bury these or place them under rocks. These can include healing spells, support notes, and other writing that speaks to Her.

Whispered promises – One of my favorite practices is to be in natural places and whisper things to trees and rocks. These might be promises to use less water, to buy less plastic, etc. You can promise to hold Her in reverence or you might promise to take on a larger project. Whispering these promises into the wind or into a piece of worn bark is simple, easy, and allows you to connect at any moment.

Listening places – Early in an initiatory process I completed (are they ever complete?), I was given a challenge to create a sit spot. This is a place you will call your own and a place you will return to regularly. I was tasked with finding a spot and sitting quietly for 10 minutes a day for 30 days to see how things changed over time. I journaled each day and I also stayed as still as possible. You'll notice that not only do you see things shift, e.g., light, animal sounds, etc., but you also begin to be a part of that place. Animals are not as startled by you, so the sounds often get louder. If you stick with this practice for a longer time, you will see the seasons change. While this is a sit spot, I also think of it as a listening place. I invite you to listen to what Gaia might offer you in your reverent stillness.

The thing to think about is that if Gaia is Mother Earth, then you are always in Her temple. You have always been a priestess or priest or some other devotee. You have always been in this relationship, for good or ill. How you cultivate this relationship now will allow it to grow into something more reciprocal and collaborative.

Communities for Gaia

And you don't have to keep Gaia all to yourself. Though your friends and family may not understand the idea of a deity, they might understand the importance of caring for Earth. If you begin to talk about how you are taking steps to support the environment, you may be able to recruit people to help you out in this work.

That said, it is also wise to work with groups and organizations already doing the work to support the environment instead of starting something else.

Clean-up days – Your community might already have groups that schedule clean-up days or trash clean-up days in your area. Some of these are related to the structure of your town or city and certain locations, e.g., the local beach, park, etc. See what you can find via online searches and news sources to see what you can join.

Donations – While getting out is helpful for Gaia, some organizations will benefit tremendously from financial contributions. Not only will these help with operating costs, but also with staffing and political lobbying efforts. I encourage you to align your donations with organizations with a proven record of taking action and who are local first as that donation will have a more significant impact.

Experiences together – I truly believe people come to help and support Gaia by experiencing Her beauty and wonder. So, get people together to see the local parks. Go on walks together or learn about the local ecology. There are often events that don't require hiking where you can learn about plants or animals. The more you can see what is already around you, the more devoted you become to protecting it.

Affinity groups – Creating circles of support will be essential in the work of being with Gaia. In activist circles, affinity groups[24] can be a source of connection and resourcing in difficult times. As I have used and learned to use this system, the basic premise is to have a group of people connected through a common cause. For example, you might create a circle of people devoted to Gaia and supporting Her. This circle might meet regularly to talk about your concerns and worries. The goal is to have a place to be heard and held. This is not necessarily a place where you will have problem solved. You might be able to ask each other for support and do magick together, but this depends on what you agree is the purpose.

Community is essential for the work of earth activism. There are no standout individuals who are going to save us all from the impact of humans on the planet. It will take many people coming together to work together.

Chapter 7

Looking toward the Future

In choosing our story, we not only cast our vote of influence over the kind of world future generations inherit, but we also affect our own lives in the here and now. When we find a good story and fully give ourselves to it, that story can act through us, breathing new life into everything we do. When we move in a direction that touches our heart, we add to the momentum of deeper purpose that makes us feel more alive. A great story and a satisfying life share a vital element: a compelling plot that moves toward meaningful goals, where what is at stake is far larger than our personal gains and losses. The Great Turning is such a story.

Joanna Macy, *Active Hope: How to Face the Mess We're in without Going Crazy*

The future looks bleak for Earth. There is a real urgency about how things are changing and people's lives will be impacted. This will require something from each of us, even if we don't realize it or want to take that on. But take it on; we must. As Alice Walker has written, we are the ones we've been waiting for.

Caring for Ourselves

In her book, *Pleasure Activism,* adrienne maree brown speaks of how our disconnection from our bodies impacts how we can arrive at the work of activism. We make choices out of fear when we are unaware of how to notice what invigorates us and what feels in alignment. These choices can lead to less desirable outcomes, dissatisfaction, burnout, and stagnation.

I want to encourage the idea that we can enjoy activism because we are aware of ourselves. We become aware of ourselves by caring for these precious bodies, which are also of the earth. We are beings and animals that interact and impact and create change. While caring for your body is something only you can define, I might offer some basics to consider as a foundation.

- **Nourishing foods** – Making a practice of giving your body foods that energize you will support you in any work in the world. Sitting and contemplating what feels right is the first step to bringing your body what it is asking for. It is undoubtedly a practice to drop into your body to hear from it and it is well worth the exploration.
- **Movement** – You do not need to run ultramarathons or lift heavy weights to move your body in a nourishing way. Walking or swimming or dancing from a seated position are all ways to give yourself attention, flexibility, and strength. We are somatic creatures who move in the world. We can move with change and through struggle by moving our bodies.
- **Rest** – I am the first person to tell you that I thought 'true' activism and Gaia support looked like doing all that I could until I could not physically do anymore. I was a keen supporter of 'I will rest when I'm dead.' But this helps no one. This does not help a movement and it certainly doesn't help you. It creates burnout and resentment. Instead, make time for rest. Make time for stepping back from action. Sleep. Do things that are slow and gentle. Zone out. Stretch. Lay in the sun and shade. Move away from the mentality that you have to DO all the time. Let capitalism's lie of 'productivity is a measure of your value' fall away from your life.
- **Play** – There will be plenty of moments where things can feel challenging, if not impossible. By making space for play and joy, you will continue to feel engaged. You

cannot work all the time. You should not work all the time. This is why community and groups are essential. Everyone needs to step back and away to replenish. You need to find ways to laugh and sing and dance.

- **Safe places and people** – It is wise to find safe places of support. Whether this is a group of friends, an affinity group, or some other gathering place, you need to know you can collapse and be human. You need a place where you can scream, make mistakes, and not be discarded for imperfection.
- **Devotional work** – While we've already talked about how to work with Gaia, you can expand this into devotion work for yourself. You might take time to meditate or to connect with nature in a way that makes sense to you. When you connect with some divine experience, it creates perspective and can remind you that you are a part of something greater.

I do not want this to land as 'do self-care.' And that is necessary to continue to do work that is in service to the planet. But care is also something that should be done in community. Yes, care for yourself, but also create a community in which care is supported. Have people you reach out to when you need help, but also be the help someone else needs. The more we can learn to rely on each other, the more we will lighten the load of this work.

Community care includes sharing resources and stepping in for someone else when they need to rest. It is speaking up to say that you need to step back and having request honored and held well. It is creating a culture in which everyone gets a chance to be joyous in this work.

Creating Sustainable Groups

One of the truths about group work is that it is challenging. When you gather people together, you gather stories and perspectives. Not everyone will agree all the time. Not everyone is at their best. Not everyone likes each other, even if they have similar values. But since we need each other, how can we create sustainable groups?

Agreements

When bringing a group together, it will help to create a set of agreements around everything. It can seem cumbersome, but it will help to have systems in place before things are tough versus trying to come up with ideas in a tense moment.

- What are we focused on?
- How will we communicate? How frequently?
- How often will we meet?
- What kinds of things will we do together?
- What do we do during a conflict?
- Who is in the group? How do we add new people? Do we?

Vision and values

A clear idea of what is important to the group will be a helpful guide. Of course, things can change and shift. Priorities might need to adjust. One of the first meetings of a group can include creating a list of values that inform the overall vision. Sort of like a mission statement; you can write this up as a group and refer to it when you are in conflict or unsure of what to do next.

Feedback

Since there are points when you may need to offer feedback to someone else or you want to give feedback about something your group did together, it helps to have a process in place. This might look like a clear expectation of how feedback will be given and received, how quickly it needs to be given, what feedback should and should not include, if consent is needed before giving feedback, etc. Again, the more you outline this, the more easily you can put your ideas into action when the situation arises.

Regular check-ins

The more you can build rapport and connections in a group through consistent communication; the more sustainable the group will be. While life certainly has its moments when things can get off track, it is wise to commit to a way of checking in regularly. This doesn't have to be just check-ins about the goals. It should also be check-ins to see where people are in their lives and how this impacts them. Remember, much work with Gaia and earth activism is about building relationships, so your group will need to focus on that too.

Conflict resolution

If there is one thing a group can know for sure, it's that conflict will happen. It will occur at times when you least expect it and often at times of stress. Ideally, you will have a process to navigate this before you need to. A basic template might be to start by addressing conflict between two people with those two people working it out as they can. If they cannot, then the group might step in to help. And if that doesn't work, then a mediator can be helpful.

I want to remind you that conflict is not bad; it is normal and expected. Groups can grow stronger through the way they approach conflict. The repair process allows for a stronger understanding of each other and a reassurance that conflict will not break a group apart.

Cultivating Radical Hope

How do you have hope in a burning world? How do you continue to believe in better in the presence of bad news? I think the answer lies in our imagination. It also lies in the continued commitment to what we believe is important.

I have learned in my life that hope is hard when faced with the unknown. Our bodies are hardwired to find the negative in the world around us. It's how we survive and it's how we stay safe. But this negativity bias also keeps us from taking more significant steps and can stifle our creative selves.

Just for a moment, I encourage you to think about people whose work you admire in the world. Think about how they have changed things for the better, brought stuff out of the shadows, and faced the most difficult times. Do you think for one minute they always knew what the next step was? Do you think they understood their place in the timeline of history? Probably not. They were just doing what they thought was right, day after day. They were also afraid and confused and tired. And yet, they moved ahead. They moved on. They gathered people around them.

They were fueled by hope. Hope for the possibility of more. After all, hope is not a definable outcome. It is a feeling of possibility. It is trusting that there is more to come. It is believing that even if you don't know how, you know something is right around the corner. You understand that each right decision you make will inform the future and impact whatever comes next.

Hope is a thing of wonder and possibility. It is not a list of To Dos. It is not an endpoint. It is the light you see far off in the distance that you keep moving toward, despite no reason to do so.

I am a recklessly hopeful, aggressively hopeful person. This does not always come out as optimism, but it does come out of the idea that a new day is already on its way. Why not welcome it? Why not appreciate the surprise it is likely to offer? Why not believe that it has ideas I haven't conceptualized yet?

Moving toward something new means you don't know what it looks like. This means you don't know what it will feel like or when it even arrives. You can wake up each day hopeful. You can continue to show up and do and be ready for things you could never imagine.

Hope is a muscle, to be sure. It is a practice of showing up repeatedly despite things being awful and messy. But the more you lean into hope, the more you will do along the way.

Hope is a guiding light and a push from behind. Hope is a prayer that you said so many years ago, a prayer that is answered each time you return to what is important. Hope is also the thing that others are seeking too – and when you live in hope, you become that light for others to follow and to take as a sign that there is more to come.

Looking Forward without Attachment

I genuinely believe in the idea that the future is something we can't predict entirely. There are trends, there are studies, and there are expectations. But I was surprised anyway. Humans are unpredictable – sometimes in wonderful and awful ways. The world is so complex, that I cannot begin to assume I know how anything will happen.

So, I invite you to live in this world and into this relationship with Gaia without attachment to the outcome. Just as love is not love when it relies on control to feel safe or comfortable, your attachment to things happening in a certain way is stifling.

Attachment can distract you from other possibilities, ideas, and plans that might work better. Having a specific, quantifiable goal in mind makes a lot of sense in the business world, but in creating a new world, I encourage you to think bigger and wider. Surrender to the possibility that you don't know everything, but you can follow what is presenting itself along the way to wherever you are going.

This is easier said than done, so here are some hints to help:

- **Get curious** – Ask more questions. See if there is something you're not looking at. Look at it from another perspective. Get back to the basics and work forward again.

- **Keep breathing –** When you notice yourself holding your breath, it's likely because you're attached to the outcome. Take a deep breath. Notice any tension in your body and ask yourself if you might be attached.
- **Be present –** The best way to loosen the grip of attachment is to come back to the present moment. This will help you stay out of trying to fix the past or trying to predict the future. A quick way to become present is to hum to yourself until your heart rate slows down. You can also practice meditation to help you create a familiar state of presence.

When you are inspired by something and are fired up about something, it is easy to think that THIS is how things need to happen. THIS is what needs to occur and if not, then we did something wrong. This is what makes earth activism frustrating at points. You do all this work and the thing you thought would happen doesn't. It's demoralizing.

And in thinking about that, can you begin to see why releasing attachment might be more sustainable? By shifting the possibilities, you are never stuck. You are just learning and moving onward toward something else.

Challenging Limited & Oppressive Thinking

I also want to bring in the very real challenge of your thinking. We all have biases and we have all been brought up to see the world in certain ways. We can create a more expanded view of the world through awareness and unpacking of these belief systems.

But until then, our thinking might get in the way – and we may not know it.

Before I go into the limitations of white supremacy and colonizer thinking for white folks, I would encourage you to take a breath. So many of us have grown up in a culture that has normalized certain ways of living. That you have beliefs that you want to change does not make you flawed or a bad person. You just have things to look at. You will continue to have things to look at. You will continue to unpack your beliefs and how they are oppressive and limiting.

Signs of white supremacy thinking:[25]

- Perfectionism
- Sense of urgency
- Defensiveness
- Quantity over quality
- Worship of the written word
- Paternalism
- Either/or thinking
- Power hoarding
- Fear of open conflict
- Individualism
- Progress is Bigger, More
- Objectivity
- Right to Comfort

When you see these things show up in the groups you are in or in your thinking, it is a sign to stop and think about the impact. As you can see, we've already talked about many of these in building a relationship with Gaia and actively working on environmental causes.

What I will add is that white supremacy thinking is directly impacting the environment by causing people to act without thought or to create groups that are not effective. The thing I take away more from recognizing and continuing to unpack my thinking is that any work I do in the world needs to be questioned. Any reactions I have need to be examined. Am I acting out of these thinking patterns? If so, how can I redirect?

How can I seek out resources to help me cultivate and maintain awareness?

In addition to white supremacy thinking, I have also brought up the colonizer mindset and its impact on the planet. When we think we are 'entitled' to the world and its resources, we take more than we need. We reduce what is available for the whole and hoard the power ownership can provide.

The future requires humans to come together to make change, to create conditions which everyone can thrive. For people to thrive, the planet will need resources and clean water. Earth will need to be at a livable temperature. It will need to have sea levels that keep cities habitable, etc.

We are all in this together, so how can we do this in a way that serves humankind as a whole? We do this by caring for ourselves, by creating groups of trust, by cultivating hope, and by challenging limiting thinking.

Together, we can and will support the health of Gaia. We must.

Conclusion

> *Unceasingly the Earth-Mother manifested her gifts on Her surface and accepted the dead into Her body. In return She was revered by all mortals. Offerings to Gaia of honey and barley cake were left in a small hole in the earth before plants were gathered. Many of Her temples were built near deep chasms where yearly the mortals offered sweet cakes into Her womb. From within the darkness of her secrets, Gaia received their gifts.*
> Charline Spretnak *Lost Goddesses of Early Greece,* (pp 48-49)

Gaia is a being that offers us grace and comfort, even in the darkest of times. She is a being who created the conditions for our arrival and our experience as humans. She is a goddess of all and a goddess of birthing the necessary unknown.

By building a solid and reciprocal relationship with Her, we can honor Her wonder and Her magick daily. By recognizing our role in the community, we can nourish ourselves and the beauty of the natural world.

It is easy to linger in the overwhelm. It is a reflex to think of ourselves as small and unimportant, alone in stopping the ever-growing list of destruction. It is the lie that is told to us again and again.

But you are not alone. We are not alone.

I encourage you to write a spell to yourself, a promise to yourself to remember the beauty of this world and the beauty of yourself. Return to this poem, this prayer, this spell whenever you are close to losing hope. Remember, you are here for a reason. You are born of your ancestors and you are being called by your descendants. They know you are wise and they are grateful for your heartbeats. You are made for these times.

Gaia, wondrous one, spell of our living and song of our bones,
Gaia, creatrix, magick of becoming and belonging
Gaia, Mother Earth and soft promise of moss and saltwater
From the mountains to the desert
From the green to the dry grasses
From the wild run of the cheetah to the quiet of a snail
From the depth of water tables and hidden rocks
All that is seen and yet undiscovered
I honor you in all of these moments
I honor you in all of the mysteries
Let me surrender my curiosity and my wisdom to you

Let me come together with others to hold your hands,
As you have held ours,
As you will continue to hold.
Hail Gaia.
Hail Mother Earth.

Endnotes

1. I use 'Her' as the pronoun Earth and Gaia for consistency across this text. However, I also believe that deities are beyond gender, so if you feel more comfortable with another pronoun (or none), I encourage you to do so.
2. I use 'godds' to offer a more gender-full experience of deities.
3. https://en.wikipedia.org/wiki/Demeter#:~:text=In%20ancient%20Greek%20religion%20and,the%20fertility%20of%20the%20earth
4. https://musingmestiza.com/2015/10/17/gaia-in-hesiods-theogony-tormented-tomentor-submissive-and-insurgent/
5. Note: Since there are many translations, I chose one translation for the stories to create consistency of context and spelling in this section.
6. https://theconversation.com/scientists-finally-have-an-explanation-for-the-gaia-puzzle-99153
7. https://www.nature.com/articles/d41586-019-01969-y
8. https://www.brookes.ac.uk/geoversity/publications/an-analysis-of-the-impact-of-the-gaia-theory-on-ecology-and-evolutionary-theory/#:~:text=The%20Gaia%20theory%20also%20predicted,as%20a%20self%2Dregulatory%20system
9. https://www.nature.com/articles/d41586-019-01969-y
10. https://engagethechain.org/top-us-food-and-beverage-companies-scope-3-emissions-disclosure-and-reductions
11. https://www.earthday.org/5-terrifying-climate-change-facts-scare-halloween/
12. https://www.nature.com/articles/d41586-021-01143-3
13. https://agupubs.onlinelibrary.wiley.com/doi/full/10.1029/2020GL087291

14. https://www.merriam-webster.com/dictionary/anthropomorphic
15. https://en.wikipedia.org/wiki/Earth_Day
16. https://www.earthday.org/history/
17. https://rebellion.global/about-us/
18. https://www.rainforest-alliance.org/about/
19. https://www.rainforestinfo.org.au/deep-eco/Joanna%20Macy.htm
20. https://www.bbc.com/news/science-environment-58508001
21. https://organicgrowersschool.org/ethical-foraging-responsibility-and-reciprocity/#:~:text=Ethical%20foraging%20is%20an%20ongoing,those%20who%20came%20before%20us
22. Of course, keep buying books from authors you love (hint, hint) and supporting local businesses that source their products from small entrepreneurs.
23. I learned this practice from my dear friend and co-facilitator, horizon.
24. https://localcircles.org/2012/05/17/what-is-an-affinity-group/#:~:text=An%20affinity%20group%20is%20a,inspiration%2C%20motivation%2C%20and%20fun
25. https://www.thc.texas.gov/public/upload/preserve/museums/files/White_Supremacy_Culture.pdf

Appendix A: Resources

BOOKS

brown, adrienne maree. *Emergent Strategy: Shaping Change, Changing Worlds*

brown, adrienne maree. *Pleasure Activism: The Politics of Feeling Good*

Kimmerer, Robin Wall. *Braiding Sweetgrass: Indigenous Wisdom, Scientific Knowledge and the Teachings of Plants*

Lovelock, James. *Gaia: A New Look at Life on Earth*

Lovelock, James. *The Revenge of Gaia: Earth's Climate Crisis & The Fate of Humanity*

Lovelock, James. *The Vanishing Face of Gaia: A Final Warning*

Macy, Joanna. *Active Hope: How to Face the Mess We're in Without Going Crazy*

Macy, Joanna. *Coming Back to Life: The Updated Guide to the Work that Connects*

Macy, Joanna. *World As Lover, World as Self: Courage for Global Justice and Ecological Renewal*

Seed, John and Macy, Joanna. *Thinking Like a Mountain: Towards a Council of All Beings*

WEBSITES

350.org – www.350.org

Earth Day Network – www.earthday.org

Earth Activist Training – www.earthactivisttraining.org

Extinction Rebellion (XR) – https://rebellion.global/

Environmental Defense Fund (EDF) – www.edf.org

Greenpeace – www.greenpeace.org

National Resources Defense Council (NRDC) – www.nrdc.org

Rainforest Alliance – www.rainforest-alliance.org

Reclaiming Witchcraft – www.reclaiming.org

Sierra Club Foundation – www.sierraclub.org
Spiral Dance Ritual – www.reclaimingspiraldance.org
The Nature Conservancy – www.nature.org
World Wildlife Federation (WWF) – www.worldwildlife.org

Bibliography

Baring, Anne. and Cashford, Jules. *The Myth of the Goddess: Evolution of an Image*

Burkert, Walter. *Green Religion*

Evelyn-White, H G. translator. *Hesiod's Homeric Hymns, Epic Cycle*

Goodrich, Norma Lorre. *Priestesses*

Graves, Robert. *The Greek Myths*

Guiley, Rosemary Ellen. *Witches and Witchcraft*

Hamilton, Edith. *Mythology*

Hamilton, Virginia. *In the Beginning: Creation Stories from Around the World*

Lefkowitz, Mary R. *Women in Greek Myth.*

Monaghan, Patricia. *Goddesses & Heroines*

Spretnak, Charlene. *Lost Goddesses of Early Greece*

West, M.L. translator. *Hesiod's Theogony and Works and Days*

About the Author

Irisanya is a priestess and teacher in the Reclaiming tradition and has taught classes and camps worldwide, including in the US, Canada, UK, and Australia. She was initiated into the tradition in 2014. She blogs at *Patheos – Charged by the Goddess* and is a regular contributor to *Pagan Dawn*. You can find out more at www.irisanyamoon.com.

Books by Irisanya Moon

Pagan Portals: Reclaiming Witchcraft
Pagan Portals: The Norns – Weavers of Fate & Magick
Pagan Portals: Aphrodite – Goddess of Love & Beauty & Initiation
Pagan Portals: Iris – Goddess of the Rainbow & Messenger of the Godds

Practically Pagan: An Alternative Guide to Health & Well-being

Earth Spirit: Honoring the Wild – Reclaiming Witchcraft & Environmental Activism

Other books in the *Earth Spirit* series

Belonging to the Earth
Nature Spirituality in a Changing World
Julie Brett
978-1-78904-969-5 (Paperback)
978-1-78904-970-1 (ebook)

Confronting the Crisis
Essays and Meditations on Eco-Spirituality
David Sparenberg
978-1-78904-973-2 (Paperback)
978-1-78904-974-9 (ebook)

Eco-Spirituality and Human-Animal Relationships
Through an Ethical and Spiritual Lens
Mark Hawthorne
978-1-78535-248-5 (Paperback)
978-1-78535-249-2 (ebook)

Healthy Planet
Global Meltdown or Global Healing
Fred Hageneder
978-1-78904-830-8 (Paperback)
978-1-78904-831-5 (ebook)

Honoring the Wild
Reclaiming Witchcraft and Environmental Activism
Irisanya Moon
978-1-78904-961-9 (Paperback)
978-1-78904-962-6 (ebook)

Saving Mother Ocean
We all need to help save the seas!
Steve Andrews
978-1-78904-965-7 (Paperback)
978-1-78904-966-4 (ebook)

The Circle of Life is Broken
An Eco-Spiritual Philosophy of the Climate Crisis
Brendan Myers
978-1-78904-977-0 (Paperback)
978-1-78904-978-7 (ebook)

Ancient Wisdom, Modern Hope
Relearning Environmental Connectiveness
James T. Powers
978-1-78279-244-4 (Paperback)
978-1-78279-245-1 (ebook)

Beyond Sustainability
Authentic Living at a Time of Climate Crisis
978-1-80341-160-6 (Paperback)
978-1-80341-161-3 (ebook)

MOON
BOOKS

MOON BOOKS
PAGANISM & SHAMANISM

What is Paganism? A religion, a spirituality, an alternative belief system, nature worship? You can find support for all these definitions (and many more) in dictionaries, encyclopaedias, and text books of religion, but subscribe to any one and the truth will evade you. Above all Paganism is a creative pursuit, an encounter with reality, an exploration of meaning and an expression of the soul. Druids, Heathens, Wiccans and others, all contribute their insights and literary riches to the Pagan tradition. Moon Books invites you to begin or to deepen your own encounter, right here, right now.
If you have enjoyed this book, why not tell other readers by posting a review on your preferred book site.

Recent bestsellers from Moon Books are:

Journey to the Dark Goddess

How to Return to Your Soul

Jane Meredith

Discover the powerful secrets of the Dark Goddess and transform your depression, grief and pain into healing and integration.

Paperback: 978-1-84694-677-6 ebook: 978-1-78099-223-5

Shamanic Reiki

Expanded Ways of Working with Universal Life Force Energy

Llyn Roberts, Robert Levy

Shamanism and Reiki are each powerful ways of healing; together, their power multiplies. *Shamanic Reiki* introduces techniques to help healers and Reiki practitioners tap ancient healing wisdom.

Paperback: 978-1-84694-037-8 ebook: 978-1-84694-650-9

Pagan Portals – The Awen Alone

Walking the Path of the Solitary Druid

Joanna van der Hoeven

An introductory guide for the solitary Druid, *The Awen Alone* will accompany you as you explore, and seek out your own place within the natural world.

Paperback: 978-1-78279-547-6 ebook: 978-1-78279-546-9

A Kitchen Witch's World of Magical Herbs & Plants

Rachel Patterson

A journey into the magical world of herbs and plants, fi lled with magical uses, folklore, history and practical magic. By popular writer, blogger and kitchen witch, Tansy Firedragon.

Paperback: 978-1-78279-621-3 ebook: 978-1-78279-620-6

Medicine for the Soul
The Complete Book of Shamanic Healing
Ross Heaven
All you will ever need to know about shamanic healing and how to become your own shaman...
Paperback: 978-1-78099-419-2 ebook: 978-1-78099-420-8

Shaman Pathways – The Druid Shaman
Exploring the Celtic Otherworld
Danu Forest
A practical guide to Celtic shamanism with exercises and techniques as well as traditional lore for exploring the Celtic Otherworld.
Paperback: 978-1-78099-615-8 ebook: 978-1-78099-616-5

Traditional Witchcraft for the Woods and Forests
A Witch's Guide to the Woodland with Guided Meditations and Pathworking
Mélusine Draco A Witch's guide to walking alone in the woods, with guided meditations and pathworking.
Paperback: 978-1-84694-803-9 ebook: 978-1-84694-804-6

Wild Earth, Wild Soul
A Manual for an Ecstatic Culture
Bill Pfeiffer
Imagine a nature-based culture so alive and so connected, spreading like wildfire. This book is the first flame...
Paperback: 978-1-78099-187-0 ebook: 978-1-78099-188-7

Naming the Goddess
Trevor Greenfield
Naming the Goddess is written by over eighty adherents and scholars of Goddess and Goddess Spirituality.
Paperback: 978-1-78279-476-9 ebook: 978-1-78279-475-2

Shapeshifting into Higher Consciousness
Heal and Transform Yourself and Our World with Ancient Shamanic and Modern Methods
Llyn Roberts
Ancient and modern methods that you can use every day to transform yourself and make a positive difference in the world.
Paperback: 978-1-84694-843-5 ebook: 978-1-84694-844-2